Learn to Navigate

An introduction for all ages

FIFTH EDITION

Basil Mosenthal

Adlard Coles Nautical

London

Acknowledgements

Charts and extracts from tidal publications have been reproduced by permission
of The Controller of H. M. Stationery Office, the UK Hydrographic Office (www.ukho.gov.uk),
and Reeds Nautical Almanac.

Note: charts reproduced in this book which have been adapted for instruction may be neither
correct nor up-to-date. They must not be used for navigation.

Photographs of GPS navigation equipment on pages 65 and 66 are courtesy of Garmin Limited.
Title page picture is courtesy of
Sea Chest Nautical Bookshop, Plymouth.
Photo on page 17 is courtesy of John Dodds Studios, Bournemouth.

Special thanks to Robert Dearn and Sea Chest Nautical Bookshop
for their considerable help in updating this edition.
Also to Richard Mortimer for his assistance with electronics.

This edition published 2007 by Adlard Coles Nautical
an imprint of A & C Black (Publishers) Ltd
38 Soho Square, London W1D 3HB

Copyright © Basil Mosenthal 1995, 1998, 2001, 2004, 2007

ISBN 978 0 7136 8263 2
First edition published by Adlard Coles Nautical 1995
Second edition 1998
Third edition 2001
Fourth edition 2004
Fifth edition 2007

A CIP catalogue record for this book is available from
the British Library.

This revised and updated edition designed, illustrated and typeset in 11/14pt Caslon
by Robert Mathias, Publishing Workshop, London

Printed and bound in Singapore by KHL Printing

CONTENTS

LEARN TO NAVIGATE

An introduction for all ages

Welcome to navigation – and may you enjoy it! Because it is a highly satisfying skill, and not very difficult to learn.

The successful navigator is merely one who follows the simple procedures, works carefully, and makes the best of their experience.

It may sometimes seem that electronic gadgets such as GPS and electronic plotters will soon take over and that sailors will no longer have to know basic navigation. Certainly GPS is now an important part of small craft navigation. It is here to stay and we shall be having a look at it, at least in outline, in Chapter 15.

- Although almost every boat now carries a GPS and this equipment is extremely reliable – it is not infallible. How do you get home if your GPS breaks down?

- You may have an excellent plotter, but close inshore with lots of traffic and buoys is not the moment to be glued to the screen and not keeping a look out around you.

- And above all, a GPS cannot be used effectively without understanding the first principles of navigation. So this is where we shall start.

ABOUT THIS BOOK

As the subtitle says, this book is only an introduction to navigation. It aims to be very simple, and includes some short cuts. It is not a textbook for passing exams.

Anyone who goes afloat should learn something about navigation, whether or not they want to become a navigator. It adds a lot of interest when going to sea, and if the skipper or the navigator is put out of action, it is good to have someone else aboard who can take the boat safely back to port.

For those who want to learn how to navigate, there is enough in this book to get you started, at least in coastal waters. And the more practice you can get afloat the better. In due course you may want to get formal instruction so that you can fill in any gaps in your knowledge, and perhaps sit for one of the RYA qualifications. It is worth noting that, despite the ever increasing use of GPS and electronic plotters, the RYA still require a knowledge of basic navigation in their exams, and are likely to do so for a long time yet.

Navigating a power boat is not very different from navigating a sailing yacht, and this book is intended for both power and sail. But, for simplicity's sake, we do sometimes talk about 'sailing' or 'going for a sail'.

Finally, it should go without saying that girls make excellent navigators. But too much use of 'he' or 'she' in a book becomes tedious for the reader, so we offer due apologies for referring to the navigator throughout this book as 'he'.

CHAPTER 1

Charts

*Charts are the basis of safe navigation, and are even
more essential to the sailor than a road map is to the
motorist. Therefore your first approach to navigation
is to find out what kinds of charts are available –
and to understand what you see on them.*

A chart can show a large scale plan of a harbour, a stretch of coastline, or an entire
ocean. In the UK there are two types of chart: those published by the Admiralty and
the commercial charts published by Stanford and Imray which are specially produced
for yachtsmen and small craft, and cover most of the areas frequently used by yachtsmen.

Standard Admiralty Charts cover virtually the whole world and have a reputation for
accuracy and detail. There are also Admiralty Leisure Charts, which cover the most popular
sailing areas in the UK, the Channel Islands and some parts of France. These are in two
formats. Admiralty Leisure Editions are standard Admiralty charts printed on high-wet-
strength paper and folded to approximately A4 size. There is also a growing range of
Admiralty Leisure Folios covering the most popular areas and each contains 12 – 20
charts of A2 size (approx 600mm x 420mm), which is a good size for a chart table.

Both Admiralty Leisure Charts and commercial charts show, on their reverse side, a
good deal of general information such as radio channels, details of weather forecasts,
and safety information. Some charts also have details of local harbours and tidal
conditions.

*You may also see Admiralty charts on CD ROM for display on a screen. But although this
arrangement may look interesting, it need not concern you until you have acquired more
experience. To start with, all navigators must be able to work efficiently on a basic paper
chart. Take an opportunity to look at these different types of chart and talk to people who
use them. As a navigator you may develop a preference, but you should learn to work
with any type of chart.*

Abbreviations and symbols

In order to save space, numerous abbreviations and symbols are used to indicate the features on a chart. Many are self explanatory but some need to be learned.

Abbreviations and symbols are illustrated in full on Admiralty chart 5011 (which is in fact a booklet and worth buying). A selection of the more common ones is also included on the back of commercial charts and in nautical almanacs.

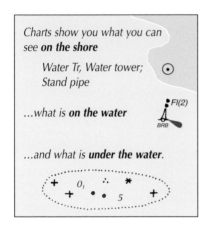

*Charts show you what you can see **on the shore***

Water Tr, Water tower; Stand pipe

*...what is **on the water***

*...and what is **under the water**.*

The very extensive range of symbols and abbreviations is a reminder of just how much information there is on most charts. Note that there are symbols indicating features on the land as well as on the water, and that the contours of the land are shown on charts. This is important for coastal navigation.

You cannot be expected to remember every symbol, and there are many that will never concern you, but being at home with charts and understanding what you see on them is an important part of being a competent navigator – and it is enjoyable!

■ *If you see something on a chart that you don't understand – look it up!*

Soundings

The figures in the chart areas covered by water are known as soundings and show the depth of water in that position. In chapter 5 we will look at how the depth of the water is affected by the rise and fall of the tide.

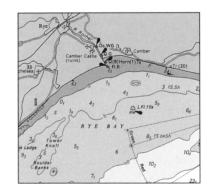

Modern charts show depths in metres, but there are still some older charts around that show depth in fathoms. Watch out for these. There are six feet in a fathom – a term some sailors still like to use.

In places you will see soundings like 3_2 which means a depth of 3.2 metres.

Take a look at the part of an Admiralty Chart on the right. Note how the colouring is giving a clue as to the depth, and the contour lines and soundings are filling in the detail. Above the 0 metre contour line (Chart Datum) the colour changes to green indicating areas that dry out when the tide is sufficiently low.

Colours

The colours used on the various types of chart vary with the publisher, but they are easy to understand. For instance on Admiralty charts the land is yellow, areas that dry out at low water are green, shallow water is blue and deeper water is white.

Scale and distance

The unit for measuring distance at sea is the *nautical mile (nm)*. This is 1,825 metres, 2,025 yards, or 1.15 statute miles, but more importantly, it is the same as *one minute of latitude*. Some large scale charts do have distance scales like road maps, but generally distance is taken from the latitude scale on the *side* of the chart. Looking at this will let you have an idea of the area covered by the chart.

One minute of latitude equals one nautical mile.

50°0′ N

Latitude and longitude

Lines of latitude and longitude are shown on all charts so that the area covered by the chart can be fitted into the overall world pattern.

Lines of *latitude* on your chart are horizontal. The Equator is Lat. 0° and the further north you go, the higher the latitude becomes. Eg Lisbon is 38° 44′ N, Falmouth is 50° 10′ N.

Lines of *longitude* are vertical, and longitude is expressed in degrees and minutes *east or west of longitude 0°*. Lines of longitude are also called *meridians*, hence long 0° is also referred to as the *Greenwich Meridian*.

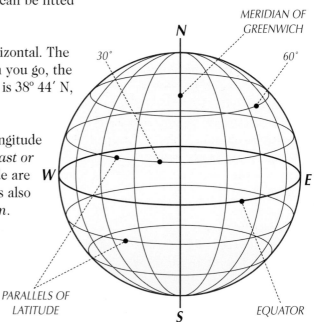

MERIDIAN OF GREENWICH

N

30°   60°

W   E

PARALLELS OF LATITUDE

S

EQUATOR

▶ *If you look at a globe you will see that lines of latitude and longitude are actually circles. But they are made to appear on charts as straight lines.*

Longitude 0°, the Greenwich Meridian, passes through the UK. For anyone navigating in the English Channel, it makes a big difference whether their longitude is E or W. A vessel whose longitude is 1°W will be near Portsmouth, while 1°E is a long way up the Channel off Dungeness.

Depths

The traveller on land needs to know where he is. But the navigator has to know where he is *and* worry about the depth of water, at least when he's sailing inshore.

■ **The chart shows what you can't see – the depth of the water, and hidden dangers such as rocks, wrecks, and sandbanks.**

Scattered among the soundings you will see abbreviations which indicate the nature of the sea bottom

For instance: S – sand, M – mud, Sh – shells.

Nowadays their only use for you is in choosing a place to anchor, when you will be hoping to find mud or sand.

Underwater dangers

Although you can always look up chart symbols that you don't understand – **you must be able to recognize the symbols that indicate underwater dangers.** A selection of the most important are shown here.

It is possible to see from the chart that some dangers are a hazard only to bigger vessels whose hulls are deeper.

As a start, it is good sense to stay clear of all rocks, wrecks and any areas where the depth of water may be uncertain and where there is potential danger.

▲ *Do not anchor in foul ground.* ▲ *A dangerous wreck.*

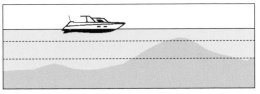

▲ *Only by looking at the chart can this vessel know that there is a sandbank ahead.*

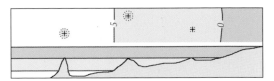

▲ *Rocks which are always visible – even at high water.*

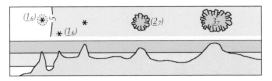

▲ *Rocks covered at high water but visible at low water.*

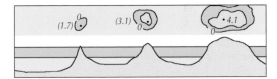

▲ *A dangerous underwater rock.*

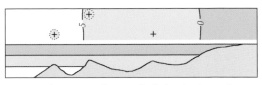

▲ *An underwater rock over which the depth is unknown, but which is considered a danger to surface navigation.*

▲ *Overfalls and tide-rips where the water is disturbed.*

Enough charts?

The navigator must make sure that there are enough charts aboard to cover the area where the boat is planning to sail. A coastal chart does not normally have detailed coverage of individual harbours.

At a pinch you could use a harbour plan in a pilot book or almanac – but, **generally, do not sail into a harbour or anchorage without a detailed chart.**

One advantage of the commercial charts is that they have inset harbour plans for the area covered by the chart. This can reduce the number of charts that need to be carried, a significant saving in cost. However these may not be on such a large scale as Admiralty harbour plans.

You also have to think about the other harbours in the area that you are not intending to visit, but where you might go if there is a change of plan – or you need to shelter from bad weather.

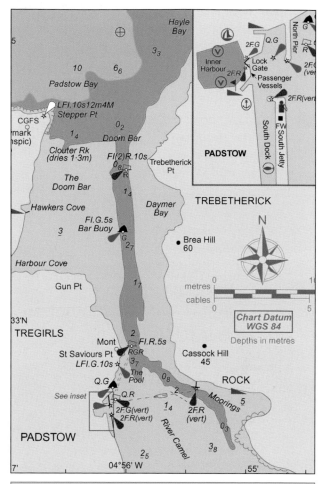

This chart from Reeds Nautical Almanac is very clear, but may not show as much detail as a regular harbour chart.

Nautical Almanacs

Nautical Almanacs are annual publications containing a variety of information for the navigator. Some of this information, such as tide tables, will change each year.

Almanacs also include much valuable detail about ports and harbours, their facilities and how to approach them.

One of the most comprehensive yachtsman's almanacs is the *Reeds Nautical Almanac* which is also available in three regional editions. There are other good almanacs, and it is a matter of choice which one you use, but every boat does need one.

CHAPTER 2

Buoys and Lights

Lighthouses and buoys are there to guide you, and sometimes to warn you. You need to know how they can help you – and why they are warning you.

Buoys

Buoys are used mainly to mark dangers or to indicate a deep water channel. The different shapes, colours and topmarks indicate why the buoy is where it is.

Beacons, which are secured into the ground (as opposed to buoys which are moored) follow the same colour scheme as buoys.

G

When you see this on the chart...

...you must know that it looks like this in the water. It marks the starboard side of a channel.

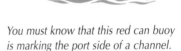

You must know that this red can buoy is marking the port side of a channel.

1. When you see a buoy on the chart, you must know what it will look like when you see it on the water.

A letter under each buoy on the chart shows its colour – <u>R</u>ed <u>G</u>reen <u>B</u>lack <u>W</u>hite <u>Y</u>ellow

2. When you do see a buoy, you must understand why it is in that position.

These marks are used to mark a deep-water channel. They may be either lit or unlit.

▲ *Port hand buoys (marking the port side of the channel when entering harbour) are **RED** can-shaped with a cylindrical topmark (if any). Lights are **RED.***

▲ *Starboard hand buoys, marking the starboard side of a channel, are **GREEN** conical with a conical topmark (if any). Lights are **GREEN**.*

Some other buoys
Their official names do help explain what the buoys are for.

▲ *ISOLATED DANGER MARK*
Black with red horizontal band.
Topmarks: 2 black spheres.
It marks a danger with clear water
round it. You can pass either side,
but not too close.

▲ *SAFE WATER MARK*
Red & white vertical stripes.
Topmark (if any): red sphere.
Often used at the approach to a
channel. It is not marking a danger
and you can pass either side of it.

▲ *SPECIAL MARK*
Yellow (shape optional).
Topmark (if any): yellow X.
Not a navigation mark but used to
indicate a special feature such
as a military exercise area.

Cardinal buoys
These take their names from the cardinal points of the compass – N, E, S, and W. They indicate the position of a danger according to where the buoy is. A west cardinal buoy is sited to the west of a danger, and so on.

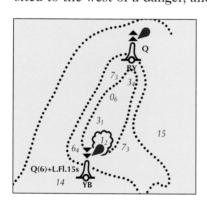

◄ *This is how Cardinal*
buoys might be sited either
side of a dangerous rock.

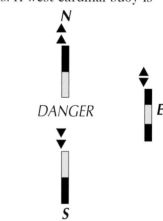

▶ *CARDINAL BUOYS*
Note the different top marks and
colours which help identify them.

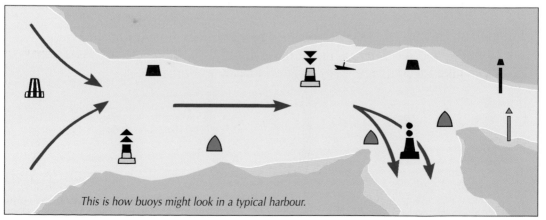

This is how buoys might look in a typical harbour.

Lights

These include lighthouses, light vessels, and lit buoys. Most light vessels are now being phased out and replaced either by very large buoys or fixed structures. On charts all lights are indicated by a purple blip (*see opposite*).

Identifying lights

The sailor must be able to distinguish one light from another. This applies equally to the lights on buoys in a channel, or to a lighthouse sighted from far out at sea.

This is made possible by lights having different *characteristics* – the colour, the type, the rhythm of their flashes and the interval between them.

This characteristic is shown on the chart alongside each light and lit buoy. For lighthouses they also show the height and the range of the light – which is the distance at which it can be seen by ships.

Types of light and rhythms

Fixed (F): can be confused with shore lights – therefore not often used.

Flashing (Fl): the period of light is much shorter than the interval between the flashes. 'Fl 10s' means one flash every ten seconds.

Group flashing: more than one flash in the pattern. 'Fl (3) 15s' means three flashes every fifteen seconds.

Occulting (Oc): the period of light is much longer than the period of dark.

Isophase (Iso): periods of light and dark are equal.

Quick flashing (Q): isophase lights with a very rapid rhythm (more than 40 flashes a minute). There are also 'Very Quick' (VQ) and 'Ultra Quick' (UQ) flashing lights.

Alternating (eg Al WR): the light shows more than one colour.

There are also further variations on these main types.

> **Point of Ardnamurchan**
> *Fl (2) 20s 55m 24M*
>
> *This is how the light at Point of Ardnamurchan on the west coast of Scotland is shown on the chart. The characteristic shows that there are two flashes every twenty seconds, the height of the light is 55 metres and the range is 24 miles.*

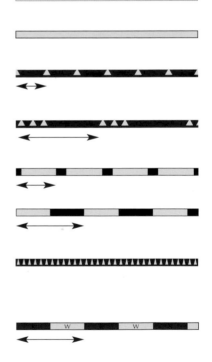

> *When you look at a lighthouse or a lit buoy on the chart you must also be able to identify that light when it flashes at you out of the darkness.*

Lights on Cardinal buoys

We now know that the topmarks on these buoys show the relative position of the danger. (Can you remember what the top marks are?) But the characteristic of the light also gives this information.

Colours of lights

Lights on buoys can be white, red, green, or yellow. Major lights are normally white, as white lights can be seen from a greater distance, but they may also show a coloured light over a limited sector to warn of a special danger. The illustration below will help to explain this.

	North
	Light: VQ or Q
West	**East**
Light: VQ (9) ev 10s	Light: VQ (3) ev 5s
or Q (9) ev 15s	or Q (3) ev 10s
	South
	Light: VQ (6) + LFl ev 10s
	or Q (6) + LFl ev 515s

▲ *Note that the number of flashes – 3, 6, and 9 are the same as the numbers on a clock.*

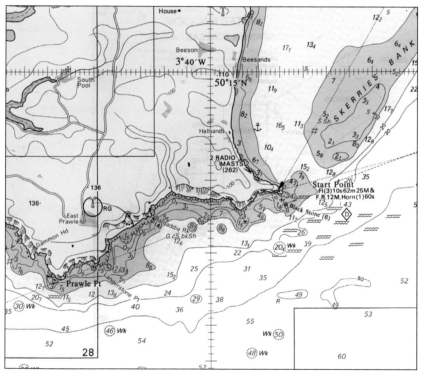

◄ *As well as its main light, Start Point shows a fixed red light over a sector to the North East, as a warning to vessels that they are approaching the Skerries Bank.*

◄ *The description on the chart alongside the light shows that the main white light flashes three times every ten seconds, and has a range of 25 miles, while the fixed red light has a range of only 12 miles.*

Sound signals

Some prominent lights have a sound signal, which is used in fog or poor visibility. This is indicated on the chart, and is usually some form of electric horn. Some buoys have a bell, operated by wave action or a gas operated whistle. They all make a dismal sound in fog!

CHAPTER 3

Your Compass

At sea you steer by your compass, when you are not heading for a mark. When you start plotting courses and bearings on a chart, these will also be related to the compass. This is a first brief look at this most important item.

Where your compass is pointing

■ You will know that there is a difference between *true north* and *magnetic north*, and that the needle in your compass will point to magnetic north.

■ The difference between true north and magnetic north is known as the *magnetic variation* (usually referred to as *variation*).

■ Magnetic variation is different in various areas of the world and there is a small annual change in each area.

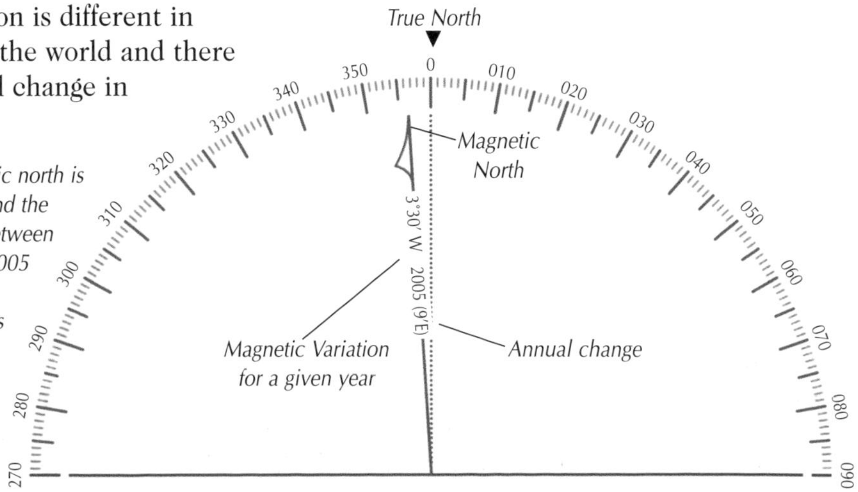

▶ *In this example magnetic north is to the west of true north and the variation (the difference between the two) is 3°30′ west in 2005 and decreases by 9′ each year. We know it decreases because the change is Easterly. As there are 60′ to a degree it will take over 6 years to change by one degree.*

The compass rose

On every chart there is at least one *compass rose* like the one below (which is – in order to make it clearer – half a compass rose). In the next chapter you will find out how to use a compass rose to plot courses and bearings on the chart. But it is shown here as a useful way of illustrating magnetic variation.

True North

Magnetic North

3°30′ W 2005 (9′E)

Magnetic Variation for a given year

Annual change

15

> *Later in this book we shall look again at the difference between True and Magnetic courses and bearings and learn how to convert them.*

The steering compass

The steering compass is marked from 0 to 360 degrees. It also shows the cardinal points, North, South, East, and West, as well as the intermediate points such as NE, SW, etc.

However, in practice, all courses and bearings are expressed in figures, not compass points. Note that three figures are always used, eg 005°, 020°, 125°.

Smaller compasses may be graduated in units of five degrees, although two degree steps are more usual. But even the most experienced helmsman can find it difficult to steer to the nearest degree or so, especially in rough weather.

Most compasses have the figures abbreviated to make them more easily read by the helmsman, so that 320 is shown as 32. But if you look at the illustration and remember that the compass is graduated round the clock from 0 to 360 degrees, this is easy to understand.

Direction

Obviously there has to be a connection between your compass and 'direction'.

At sea you can talk about the 'direction' in which you are sailing; this is your course. There is also, for instance, the 'direction' of the beacon that you can see on the shore. This is known as the bearing of the beacon.

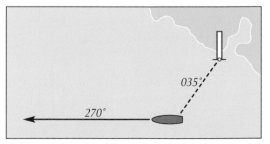

▲ *The bearing of the beacon from the boat is 035°. The boat's course is 270°.*

CHAPTER 4

Working on a Chart

Here is what you need to know before you can work successfully on a chart. We will begin by looking at the instruments that can be used.

Chart instruments

These are typical instruments for chart work.

Dividers are used for measuring distance, and these may be either bowed for using with one hand, or straight.

Parallel rulers are the traditional instrument for plotting courses and bearings but in recent years plotters such as the Portland Course Plotter shown on the right have increased in popularity. Plotters are probably more suited to the smaller chart tables of modern yachts.

Navigators have their particular favourites, and with experience you will find the type of instrument that you are happiest working with. Meanwhile, when you start to navigate, it is useful to be able to work with whatever you find to hand.

Distance

We have already said that distance at sea is measured in nautical miles and that *a nautical mile equals one minute of latitude.*

Therefore, although there are distance scales on some charts, it is the latitude scale on either *side* of the chart that is used for measuring distance.

Although depths on charts are shown in metres, kilometres are not used at sea.

Measuring distance on a chart

To measure the distance between points **A** and **B**, straddle your dividers between those points, then transfer to the scale on the side of the chart to read the distance.

Alternatively you can measure a required distance on the latitude scale and then transfer it to the chart.

The same symbol is used for nautical miles as for minutes of lat. and long. So 34 nautical miles can be written as 34′.

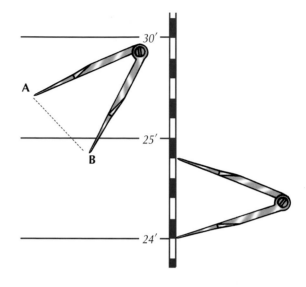

Courses and bearings

When you are working on the chart, direction is related to the compass. Courses and bearings that you plot will be measured from the *compass rose* if you use a parallel ruler, or from the circular protractor on your plotter.

We have already met this important item, but here is a further example.

◄ *The ring on the compass rose is aligned with True North, and with the lines of longitude. It is graduated clockwise from 0 to 360 degrees so that north is 000 or 360 degrees, south is 180 degrees etc. What is the variation shown on this compass rose?*

If you use a plotter you will probably find it more practical to plot all your courses and bearings in magnetic.

Plotting courses and bearings

The last chapter exlained the difference between a *course* – the direction in which the boat is heading, and a *bearing* – the direction of one object from another. When you are working on a chart, you need to be able to:

■ Measure the bearing from one point to another (for instance an object on the shore from your boat).

■ Plot the course from one point to another.

And you need to know how to work with either a parallel ruler or with a plotter.

Using a parallel ruler

With a parallel ruler you work to or from the compass rose, as the rose is aligned to True North the results will be True (T).

In this example we need to measure the course between the two buoys:

■ Line up the edge of the parallel ruler between the buoys, then by opening and closing it, carefully step it across to the centre of the nearest compass rose. Make sure that one edge is aligned exactly with the centre dot, or you will have an error.

■ Read the bearing where the edge of the ruler cuts the compass ring. But note that there are two options, according to which side of the ring you read. On the right, the course from buoy **A** to buoy **B** is **070°(T)**, from **B** to **A** it's **250°(T)**.

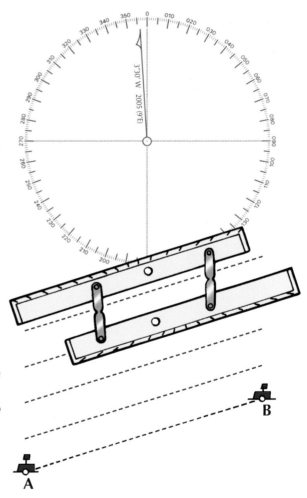

Using a parallel ruler is not difficult with a little practice.
Occasionally, when you are moving your ruler across the chart, you may feel that it has slipped. If this does happen, it is better to start again to avoid the chance of an error.

Using a plotter

With a *plotter* you do not have to use the compass rose, except to read off the magnetic variation.

Here we want to use the plotter to lay off a course of 040° from our boat at point A.

■ Set on the plotter the magnetic variation (which has been read from the compass rose).

■ Set the compass rose on the plotter to the required course, i.e. turn the dial until it shows 040° for the boat's course.

■ Line up the grid on the plotter with a convenient lat. or long. line near point A. At the same time align one edge of the plotter with point A from where you want to draw the course.

■ Draw in the line along the same edge.

> *Note: There may be a slight difference in the way various types of plotters are used. Check the instructions.*

A

Position

At sea, the position of a vessel or an object can be expressed in two ways:

■ by its latitude and longitude

■ or by means of its bearing and distance *from* a known object.

GPS and other electronic navigational equipment gives you your position in lat. and long.

▶ *The vessel's position here is described as '150° White Head 5 miles'. The bearing is given **from** the Head.*

> *At times a vessel's position may be given in approximate terms such as 'close west of the Shipshape Buoy' or 'about one mile south of White Head'. This is not sufficiently exact for navigation, but it can be useful if a quick position is needed to pass by radio in an emergency.*

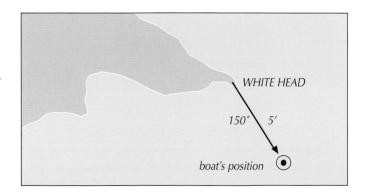

WHITE HEAD

150° 5'

boat's position ⊙

Plotting latitude and longitude

In the example below we need to find the latitude and longitude of the vessel in position **A**.

■ Line up your plotter or parallel rule on one of the chart's horizontal lines of latitude. Then, by opening and closing, move it up or down until one edge passes through the point **A**.

You can do this just as well with a plotter. Line up one side with point **A**, and at the same time, line up one of the vertical lines on the plotter with a vertical longitude line on the chart. This makes sure that the plotter is aligned to both latitude and longitude.

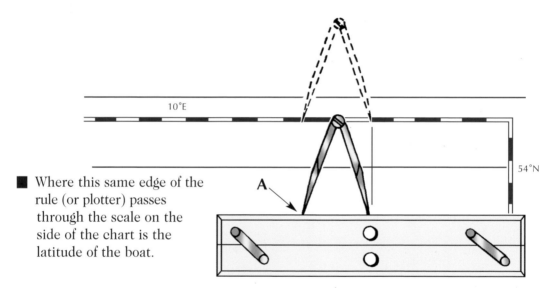

■ Where this same edge of the rule (or plotter) passes through the scale on the side of the chart is the latitude of the boat.

■ You can repeat the process by lining the ruler up vertically on a line of longitude, and then reading off the longitude at point **A** at the top of the chart.

But an easier way, as shown above, is to keep the ruler lined up for the latitude, and then position your dividers between point **A** and the nearest line of longitude.

You would follow the same drill if you wanted to plot a given latitude and longitude on the chart.

Speed

The unit of speed at sea is the knot, which is one nautical mile per hour. So that a vessel travelling at 12 knots will cover 12 nautical miles in one hour. You will sometimes hear talk of 'knots per hour', but as a knot is a unit of speed, this is incorrect.

Time – Speed – and Distance

There is obviously a relationship between these which you will often need to use.

■ Your speedometer shows that you are making 6.5 knots. The next mark is 4 miles ahead. What time will it be abeam?

■ Your log readings show that you have travelled 4.6 miles in the last 40 minutes. What is your speed?

■ Your speed is 4.2 knots. How far will you go in the next one and half hours?

These problems can be solved easily with the *Time – Speed – Distance tables* that you will find in most almanacs.

■ Use your speed and a given time to find out how far you will have travelled in that time.

■ Or start with your speed, look down the column until you see the distance you want to travel and read across to the time required to cover that distance.

■ Take a time, move across until you reach the required distance, then move up to find the speed needed to cover that distance in that time.

5½	6	6½	7	7½	8	8½	Min
0.1	0.1	0.1	0.1	0.1	0.1	0.2	1
0.2	0.2	0.2	0.2	0.2	0.3	0.3	2
0.3	0.3	0.3	0.3	0.3	0.4	0.4	3
0.4	0.4	0.4	0.4	0.5	0.5	0.6	4
0.5	0.5	0.6	0.5	0.6	0.7	0.7	5
0.6	0.6	0.7	0.6	0.8	0.8	0.9	6
0.6	0.7	0.8	0.7	0.9	0.9	1.0	7
	0.8	0.9	0.8	1.0	1.0	1.1	8
		1.0	0.9	1.1	1.2	1.3	9
			1.0	1.3	1.3	1.4	10
				1.1	1.4	1.5	1.6	11
				2	1.5	1.6	1.7	12
						7	1.8	13
								14

▶ *A typical Time, Speed, Distance table:*
– Speed is at the top and bottom
– Time (in mins) is at the side
– Distance is in the centre columns

In fact unless you are specially quick at mental arithmetic, you may find it useful to cut out the appropriate bit of the table and paste it on a card for quick reference.

Some people find a formula difficult, but if you want to use a pocket calculator, here's how:

$$\text{Distance} = \frac{\text{time} \times \text{speed}}{60 \ (\text{mins})} \qquad \text{Speed} = \frac{\text{distance} \times 60}{\text{time}} \qquad \text{Time} = \frac{\text{distance} \times 60}{\text{speed}}$$

> ***To sum up***: *This is an important chapter, and if anything is not clear, you might need to look through it again.*
>
> *Because one of the first things a navigator must learn is to be able to plot bearings, courses and positions on a chart – and do it accurately and fairly quickly. It is not difficult, if you understand what you are trying to do, and with a little practice, it can be done almost without thinking.*

CHAPTER 5

Tides – Rising and Falling

The effects of the tide can be almost as important for the sailor as the wind. And the tide is something that the navigator must know about – and always be aware of.

When we talk about tides we meet a collection of what may be new words and definitions – springs, neaps, charted depths, and so on. We will try to use as few as possible, but if you do get puzzled, there is a separate tidal section in the glossary at the end of the book.

High water and low water

The sailor sees two effects of the tide. Firstly there is the vertical rise and fall. And then there is the horizontal movement (for instance the tide pouring in and out of an estuary) which is known as the *tidal stream*. We shall deal with this in the next chapter.

high water

low water

You will have been on the shore or looking out over a harbour and been aware that the tide was 'in' at high water or 'out' at low water.

■ Normally the difference in time between *high water* (or high tide) and *low water* is a little over six hours.

■ Therefore, in most places, there are two high waters and two low waters in about 24 hours 50 minutes.

However a few parts of the world do not conform to this tidy arrangement. In areas such as the Baltic and Mediterranean there is virtually no tide.

4 hours after high water

High water

▶ *Navigators must always know what the tide is doing!*

23

Springs and neaps

The rise and fall of the tide is caused by the effects of the moon's position in relation to the sun.

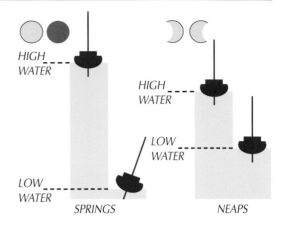

- When the moon is full, and when it is new (or two days after, to be precise), we have *spring tides*, when the rise and fall is greatest – high water is higher and low water is lower.

- Just after the first and third quarters of the moon we have *neap tides* when the rise and fall is least. It is usual to refer just to *springs* and *neaps*.

- The whole cycle from one new moon to the next takes approx. four weeks, so there are spring tides (at full and new moon) about every two weeks.

Heights and depths

When we talk about the *depth* of the water we generally mean the amount of water under our boat. And we will come across the term *actual depth*, which means what it says – the actual depth of the water in any position.

But on the next page, when you find out about *tide tables*, you will see that they refer to the *height* of the tide. However as the tide does rise and fall, it is not unreasonable to talk about its height. But height above what? – its height above *chart datum*.

Chart datum is a point of reference and is the lowest point to which the tide can be predicted to fall. Now look at the diagram below and see if you can understand how the various tidal terms fit together.

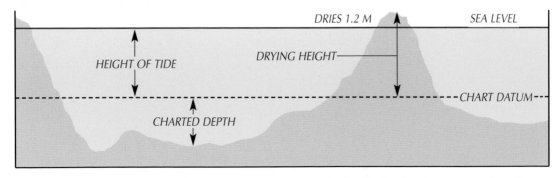

▲ Charted depth is the sounding shown on your chart. It is the least depth to be found in that position, even at low water. Height of the tide is a figure that is obtained from tide tables, and you are about to learn how to do this. You will see how this figure is added to charted depth to give you the actual depth, which is what it says.

Tide tables

These tables not only give you the time of high and low waters each day, but they also give the *height* of the tide. At the end of the chapter we will give some examples of when and why you need this.

Although there are Admiralty Tide Tables, most yachtsmen either use the tide tables in their nautical almanac or the local tide tables that are also available in many places.

The times of high and low water may vary considerably in different places within the same area, eg over a distance of 5 miles, but a set of tide tables that covered every small port and anchorage would be too bulky. So we start by having complete tables for a number of ports known as *Standard Ports*.

Below is an extract from the tide tables for Dover which is a Standard Port. For most days you will see that there are four times and four heights of the tide. On one day you might read:

0159 – 1.5	0732 – 5.5
1426 – 1.9	1948 – 5.6

The higher figures at 0732 and 1948 are the high waters and the others are the low waters.

TIME ZONE UT (GMT)
For Summer Time add ONE hour in non-shaded areas

ENGLAND, SOUTH COAST – DOVER

LAT 51°07′N   LONG 1°19′E

TIMES AND HEIGHTS OF HIGH AND LOW WATERS

MAY

	Time	m		Time	m
1 M	0712	1.0	**16** TU	0704	0.5
	1208	6.5		1143	6.9
	1921	1.1		1924	0.6
2 TU	0023	6.5	**17** W	0005	7.0
	0735	1.1		0750	0.6
	1240	6.5		1231	6.9
	1944	1.1		2010	0.6
3 W	0051	6.4	**18** TH	0055	7.0
	0759	1.2		0836	0.7
	1309	6.4		1321	6.8
	2011	1.2		2058	0.7
4 TH	0114	6.2	**19** F	0147	6.6
	0826	1.3		0923	0.9
	1334	6.2		1414	6.6
	2043	1.3		2147	0.9
5 F	0140	6.0	**20** SA	0246	6.3
	0859	1.5		1012	1.2
	1403	6.0		1512	5.9
	2120	1.5		2240	1.2
6 SA	0214	5.8	**21** SU	0350	6.0
	0938	1.7		1108	1.5
	1444	5.7		1613	6.0
	2203	1.7		2340	1.4

JUNE

	Time	m		Time	m
1 TH	0031	6.3	**16** F	0048	6.8
	0737	1.2		0833	0.6
	1250	6.4		1312	6.9
	1954	1.2		2055	0.6
2 F	0056	6.2	**17** SA	0139	6.6
	0809	1.3		0919	0.8
	1317	6.3		1401	6.7
	2029	1.3		2142	0.7
3 SA	0123	6.1	**18** SU	0232	6.4
	0844	1.4		1003	1.0
	1346	6.0		1452	6.5
	2106	1.4		2229	0.9
4 SU	0156	6.0	**19** M	0326	6.1
	0921	1.5		1049	1.3
	1424	6.0		1545	6.3
	2106	1.5		2317	1.2
5 M	0239	5.8	**20** TU	0422	5.9
	1002	1.7		1138	1.5
	1511	5.9		1642	6.0
	2232	1.7			
6 TU	0333	5.6	**21** W	0009	1.5
	1051	1.9		0522	5.6
	1611	1.8		1234	1.8

JULY

	Time	m		Time	m
1 SA	0038	6.2	**16** SU	0125	6.7
	0755	1.2		0905	0.7
	1258	6.4		1343	6.9
	2016	1.1		2126	0.6
2 SU	0106	6.2	**17** M	0209	6.5
	0830	1.3		0943	0.9
	1328	6.4		1428	6.7
	2053	1.2		2205	0.8
3 M	0138	6.2	**18** TU	0255	6.3
	0906	1.3		1020	1.1
	1403	6.3		1515	6.4
	2103	1.3		2244	1.2
4 TU	0216	6.1	**19** W	0344	6.0
	0943	1.4		1058	1.5
	1444	6.2		1604	6.1
	2210	1.4		2327	1.5
5 W	0302	6.0	**20** TH	0438	5.7
	1026	1.6		1143	1.8
	1536	6.1		1700	5.8
	2257	1.6			
6 TH	0359	5.8	**21** F	0017	1.9
	1116	1.7		0539	5.4
	1636	5.9		1241	2.1

AUGUST

	Time	m		Time	m
1 TU	0117	6.4	**16** W	0222	6.4
	0848	1.1		0943	1.2
	1340	6.6		1441	6.5
	2111	1.0		2205	1.2
2 W	0153	6.4	**17** TH	0306	6.1
	0923	1.2		1012	1.5
	1419	6.5		1526	6.1
	2147	1.2		2236	1.6
3 TH	0236	6.4	**18** F	0356	5.7
	1001	1.4		1045	1.8
	1506	6.3		1618	5.7
	2229	1.4		2315	2.0
4 F	0328	6.0	**19** SA	0455	5.4
	1049	1.6		1136	2.2
	1603	6.0		1721	5.4
	2322	1.6			
5 SA	0436	5.7	**20** SU	0020	2.3
	1151	1.8		0603	5.2
	1720	5.7		1257	2.4
				1832	5.2
6 SU	0033	1.8	**21** M	0143	2.3
	0614	5.5		0718	5.3
				1417	2.2

In UK tide tables, times are usually shown in UT (Universal Time) and one hour must be added to these times during British Summer Time (BST).

To find the depth of water anywhere at high or low water **add the figure from the tide table for that harbour (or the nearest Standard Port) to the depth shown on the chart.**

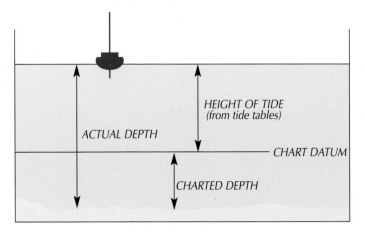

HEIGHT OF TIDE
(from tide tables)

ACTUAL DEPTH

CHART DATUM

CHARTED DEPTH

◄ *The height of the tide from the tide tables is added to the charted depth to find the actual depth.*

If you look at a tide table, the difference in height between high water and low water will tell you how much the tide is rising and falling on any day. This is known as the *rise and fall* and is useful to know. The technical term is the *range* of the tide.

Springs or Neaps?
Spring tides are higher – and lower. Neap tides are smaller.

When you go sailing, you should always know if the present tides are springs, neaps, or somewhere in between. There can be a big difference.

On most tide tables you will find a small symbol depicting a full and a new moon, and this indicates the days when spring tides are approaching. But you can also tell by the figures for the height of the tide. The biggest must be springs, and the smaller figures are neap tides.

The other ports
We now know that the ports, for which full tidal information is available, are known as *Standard Ports*. The other places for which there may not be full tide tables are known as *Secondary Ports*.

If you look up these other ports in your almanac you will see that their tides are related to the nearest *Standard Port*. The listings for these places show a *time difference*, which is added (when +) or subtracted (when -) to or from the time of HW or LW at the appropriate Standard Port. There are similar corrections for the height of the tide.

On the next page is an example.

RAMSGATE
Kent 51° 19'.48N 01°25'.60E
Standard Port DOVER (←)

Times				Height (metres)			
High Water		Low Water		MHWS	MHWN	MLWN	MLWS
0000	0600	0100	0700	6.7	5.3	2.0	0.8
1200	1800	1300	1900				
Differences RAMSGATE							
+0020	+0020	-0007	-0007	-1.8	-1.5	-0.8	-0.4

◄ This extract from Reeds Nautical Almanac shows that tidal information for Ramsgate is based on Dover as the Standard Port.

These tidal corrections are not as complicated as they may at first look.

1. You will see that there are two columns for the times of high and low water, and the corrections may depend on the time of day. However there is often little difference between the two (and there is none at Ramsgate).

2. The correction for the height of the tide also has four columns, and the letters mean:

MHWS – Mean high water springs
MHWN – Mean high water neaps
MLWS – Mean low water springs
MLWN – Mean low water neaps

Here 'mean' is used for 'average'.

All this just shows that the correction for the height of the tide will be different for high water and low water, and that the corrections during spring tides are different to those during neap tides.

For example:

Supposing you need to know the time of HW and the height of the tide at Ramsgate during the morning on a certain date.
Your almanac tells you that tidal information for Ramsgate is based on Dover.
Looking at the Dover tide tables you find:
HW is 1053 (corrected for BST) and the height is given as 6.1.
The figures also show that the tides are approaching springs.

Referring back to the Ramsgate figures above, we see that time difference for HW is +0020, and that the difference for height at high water, springs (MHWS) is -1.8.

This gives us:

HW Dover	*1053*	*6.1*
Difference	*+0020*	*-1.8*
HW Ramsgate	*1113*	*4.3*

Why do we need to know the exact depth?

As a sailor you obviously have to be concerned about the depth of the water under your boat. And you have already been warned to keep away from rocks and other dangers rather than wonder if there is enough water for you to scrape over them.

But there are places where it is safe to be in relatively shallow water, and this is why you need to be able to understand tide tables and calculate the exact height of the tide.

For instance you may be looking for a place to anchor close to the shore. You must be sure that there is enough water for you to stay afloat at low water: but you must also know the depth at high water so that you put out enough anchor chain. So you need to be able to work out the approx. depth at high water and at low water.

As harbours get more crowded, boaters increasingly seek the quieter and more remote anchorages – which may also be shallow! Or you may have found a convenient berth alongside a harbour wall, but you want to be sure that there is still enough water to stay afloat at low water.

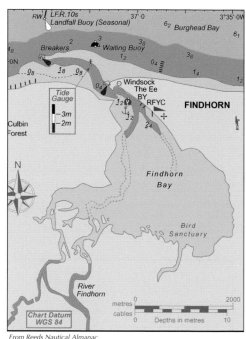

From Reeds Nautical Almanac

Too little water!

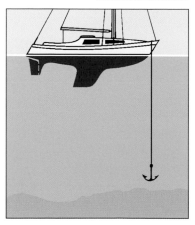

Too much water!

▲ *Findhorn on the Moray Firth is popular with local and visiting yachtsmen, but it is very shallow. To sail there you must know what the tide is doing – for instance the times of high and low water and the rise and fall of the tide.*

Finally... remember that the tide can be affected by barometric pressure and the weather – for instance continuous onshore winds can push the water up and cause higher tides than normal. Always be prepared for the tide not to obey the rules.

CHAPTER 6

Tidal Streams

Just as the tide rises and falls, there is also a horizontal movement – the tidal stream. After all, when the tide falls the water does have to go somewhere!

Although the effect of tidal streams is most obvious in rivers or at the entrance to a harbour, the charts below show that there can be a strong tidal stream in the open sea.

■ With a greater volume of water on the move, it follows that tidal streams will be stronger when the rise and fall is greatest during spring tides, and weaker during neaps.

■ The tide is said to be *flooding* as it moves towards high water, and *ebbing* as it flows out.

■ Either side of high or low water there is a period with little tidal movement known as *slack water*. It can be said that the tide is 'slack' at this time.

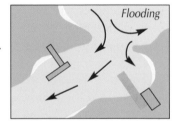

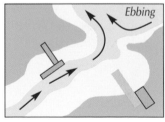

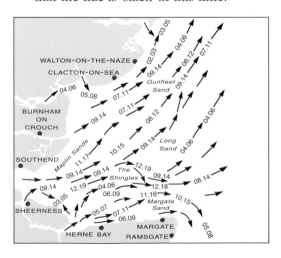

Tidal stream charts

The strength and direction of the tidal stream in any area can be shown on *tidal stream charts*. These can be found either in a series of Admiralty Tidal Atlases or in your nautical almanac. The charts are usually in series of twelve, refering to each hour before and after high water at a standard port.

◀ *4 hours after HW Sheerness (0525 after HW Dover).*

The examples on page 29 and this page are three of the twelve charts showing the tidal stream in the Thames Estuary, an area where the tides flow strongly.

These charts are based on the times of high water at Sheerness – although the figures for Dover are given as well.

■ The arrows show the tidal stream's direction. You make a rough estimation to transfer this into a compass direction.

■ The strength of the stream is usually shown by the figures near the arrows, giving the approximate rate in tenths of a knot (so that 18 means 1.8 knots). The larger of the two figures is for Springs and the other for Neaps. You need to estimate between these two figures. The strength of the stream is also shown by the relative length and thickness of the arrows.

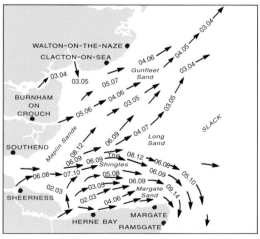

▲ *5 hours after HW Sheerness (0600 before HW Dover).*

▶ *To find out what the tidal stream is doing near position* **A** *first look up the time of high water. We reckon that it is 1 hour before HW at Devonport. The table shows that the direction is 035° and the rate is 0.5 knots at neaps or 1.2 at springs.*

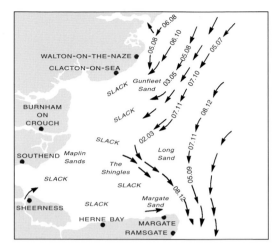

▲ *6 hours after HW Sheerness (0500 before HW Dover).*

So although the information from a tidal stream chart is very useful, it is only approximate.

Tidal information on charts

On Admiralty charts and some others there is another way of showing the tidal stream in certain positions. A letter inside a diamond ◇Ⓐ refers to a table on the chart giving the direction and strength of the tidal stream in that position. These figures are given for springs and neaps and for each hour in relation to high water at a Standard Port.

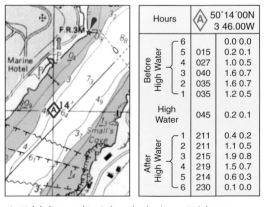

	Hours	Ⓐ	50°14′00N 3 46.00W
Before High Water	6		0.0 0.0
	5	015	0.2 0.1
	4	027	1.0 0.5
	3	040	1.6 0.7
	2	035	1.6 0.7
	1	035	1.2 0.5
High Water		045	0.2 0.1
After High Water	1	211	0.4 0.2
	2	211	1.1 0.5
	3	215	1.9 0.8
	4	219	1.5 0.7
	5	214	0.6 0.3
	6	230	0.1 0.0

▲ *Tidal diamond in Salcombe harbour. Tidal streams refer to HW at Devonport.*

The effect of the tidal stream

The effect of the tidal stream is most obvious when it is either against us or directly behind us when we are sailing in a river or the entrance to a harbour.

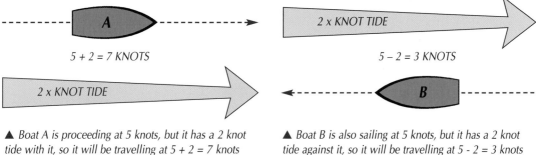

▲ Boat A is proceeding at 5 knots, but it has a 2 knot tide with it, so it will be travelling at 5 + 2 = 7 knots over the ground.

▲ Boat B is also sailing at 5 knots, but it has a 2 knot tide against it, so it will be travelling at 5 - 2 = 3 knots over the ground.

In the example above, Boat A is motoring along at its usual 5 knots, and its speedometer only shows 5 knots. But looking at the shore from the boat will show that it is going faster than that because her speed over the ground is 7 knots. You can also say that she is *making good* 7 knots.

On the other hand, aboard Boat B the speedometer will still be showing 5 knots, but a look at the shore shows that, because of the foul tide, she is actually making slow progress. In fact she is only *making good* 3 knots.

A tidal stream on the beam also has an effect.

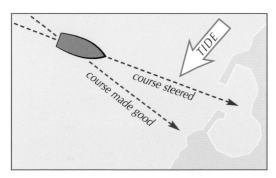

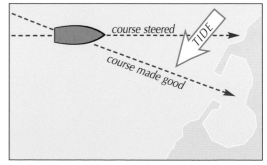

▲ Here the boat has steered for the harbour entrance but has been pushed down by the tide.

▲ This boat has steered a course to compensate for the tide, and has arrived where it wants to be.

In a later chapter you will learn how to work out and plot a course to compensate for the tidal stream.

What is the stream doing?

Always be aware of the tide's direction – and when it turns. As well as using your tide tables, keep your eyes open. There are useful signs around you of what the tide is doing.

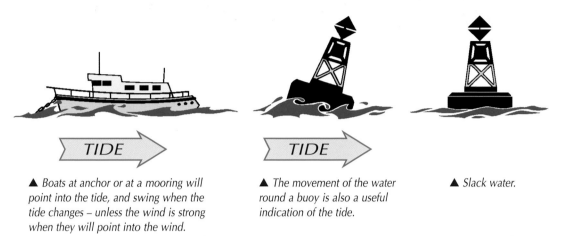

▲ Boats at anchor or at a mooring will point into the tide, and swing when the tide changes – unless the wind is strong when they will point into the wind.

▲ The movement of the water round a buoy is also a useful indication of the tide.

▲ Slack water.

Dodging the tide – or making the best of it

It pays to study tidal stream charts carefully, and see when and where the tide is strongest and weakest. There is a big difference to your progress whether you are rounding a headland with a 2 knot fair tide – or a 2 knot foul tide.

■ In a river or harbour entrance the stream often runs more strongly in the middle than at the side.

■ There may even be a favourable back eddy near the shore.

■ At slack water, the tide may often start to change near the shore before it does in the middle.

■ Get to know how the tidal streams work in the area where you sail regularly. Local knowledge like this is always useful.

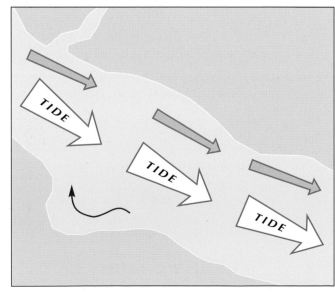

▲ This simple diagram shows the tide to be strongest in the middle of the channel and weaker near the far shore. Close to the near shore there is a weak back eddy flowing in the opposite direction to the main tide.

CHAPTER 7

Navigation Instruments

*This brief chapter is about the gear that the navigator
will be using in almost every boat, although that
most important instrument – the compass – has been
dealt with already.*

The hand bearing compass

This is an important item of equipment but we will deal it later in Chapter 9 when we discuss its use for taking bearings.

Logs

A log (not to be confused with 'log' as an abbreviation for logbook) measures distance travelled through the water.

There are various types and makes, but the visible part is normally a small electronic box with a dial, usually sited near the chart table. Often there is a repeater in the cockpit. These instruments sometimes show other information such as temperature as well as distance.

The log is activated by a sensor low down in the hull. This sensor may be electronic or a small mechanical device like a paddle wheel.

Speedometers

With any type of log the same sensor may also be used to drive a speedometer, and the same dial may be switched over to record the boat's speed. But the navigator is less concerned with speedometer readings, which are mainly useful for sail trim. If log readings are timed, as they should be, you will know how far you have travelled since your last reading and can work out your speed.

Echo sounders

An echo sounder is probably the most common item of electronic navigation equipment and you will find one in virtually every boat. In simple terms, an echo sounder measures the depth of the water by sending a sound signal to the sea bed, and then timing how long it takes to be reflected back.

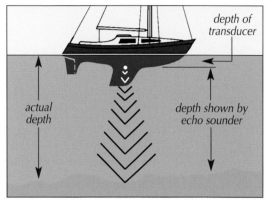

The *transducer* that transmits the sound signal is a small fitting sited low down in the hull, and out of sight.

The echo sounder measures the depth below the position of the transducer. To get the actual depth of the water (from the surface), you need to know the depth of the transducer in the hull.

■ But, for practical purposes *you use the depth shown on the echo sounder.* The navigator's most important use for an echo sounder is when entering shallow harbours and creeks, and when coming to anchor.

Lead lines

A *lead line* (pronounced 'led line') is, in fact, just a weight on the end of a marked line. It is a cheap and efficient method of measuring depth, and it cannot break down! There should always be one on board as a back up for the echo sounder.

Lead lines, which can easily be home made, are often too long. This makes them a nuisance to handle, and to stow. As you normally only use a lead line in shallow water, about 10 metres of line is quite enough.

Binoculars

There should be a pair of binoculars on board. Their particular importance to the navigator is for helping to identify buoys and other marks on the water or ashore. 7 x 50 is the best size binocular for a yacht.

Like other navigation instruments, binoculars can be easily damaged. The prisms inside can become mis-aligned if the binoculars are dropped or knocked. They should be fitted with a lanyard which should always be round the neck when in use. Binoculars should be returned to their case or stowage – not left lying around the cockpit.

CHAPTER 8

Getting Started

Navigation is said to be about 'getting a vessel from one place to another safely and efficiently'. Let's start looking at how this is done.

M uch so-called 'navigation' is done by eye, making use of shore features and navigation marks – usually buoys. Let's take an example – the western approaches to the Solent, familiar to many sailors.

Approaching from seaward, the Needles lighthouse is conspicuous. The red and white Fairway buoy (not shown on this chart) is some way out, but from the west you might head directly for the red Shingles buoy at the entrance to the Needles channel.

Plot a course to steer, then turn up into the channel. A short distance ahead is the black and yellow Bridge cardinal buoy – its topmark shows it marks a danger to the *east*, so you will leave it to *starboard*.

Then, about a mile apart there are two *port-hand* red can buoys marking the Shingles Bank and a green conical *starboard-hand* buoy. Soon after, on the *port* side, is another black and yellow cardinal buoy, its topmark indicating a danger to the *west*, so as you progress up the channel you will leave the buoy to *port*.

By this time you will be almost abeam of Hurst Point and here the channel broadens out, although there are buoys on either side.

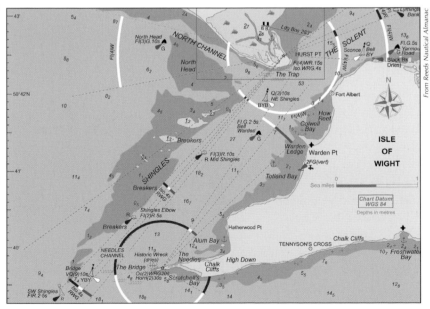

From Reeds Nautical Almanac

Pilotage

The short passage described overleaf is typical of the sort of sailing that many yachtsmen do for much of the time. It means that, when sailing inshore, more time may be spent in pilotage rather than true navigation – which could be said to start when you cannot see your next mark.

This does not mean that pilotage can be treated lightly. Boats can run aground and get into trouble more often when they are close inshore than when they are in the open sea.

When you are 'buoy hopping':

■ You still have to study the chart carefully, particularly looking for any unmarked dangers or shallow water. Unless the marks are very close together, a course should be plotted between the marks. For instance, this should be done in the example on the previous page.

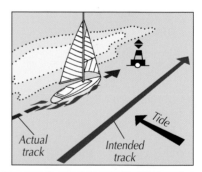

■ Buoys and lights must always be identified, especially those marking dangers. This is why you have been encouraged to recognize the various types of buoy and their significance. Every buoy carries a name or a number and its colour is shown by a letter beneath it on the chart.

■ You should always know what the tide is doing and whether there is any tidal stream where you are sailing. It is the effect of a tide on the beam that is easy to overlook. In some waters the tides can run very strongly indeed.

Look at this example:

The boat has decided to steer 035°, which looks as if it will leave the buoy to port and keep her clear of the shallow water. But no attention has been paid to the tide.

As the boat gets nearer to the buoy, the helmsman is tempted to steer to leave it close to port and not watch the compass.

And so, although the boat is still 'leaving the buoy to port', she is being swept into the shallow water.

Actual track

Intended track

Tide

These are the mistakes:

■ No one had looked at the Tidal Stream Atlas and realised that there *was* a tidal stream in that area.
■ The helmsman did not look at his compass and realise that the course needed to leave the buoy to port was getting quite different to 035°, the course ordered.
■ A glance at the echo sounder, which is always sensible near shallow water, would have shown the approaching shoal water.

Plotting and steering a course

You have learned how to plot a course from one point to another. You probably thought that this would not be necessary for short distances. But...

■ Supposing that, while you are 'buoy hopping', you run into a patch of fog and cannot see your next mark.

■ Or, at night, it is difficult to pick up the next buoy against the shore lights.

■ Or, again, you are in an area such as the Solent or the Thames Estuary, where there may be numerous buoys in sight, and you need to sure that you are heading for the right one.

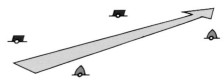

In these cases, you do have to plot a course to the next mark. Then steer that course until you sight the mark *and know it is the right one*. Steering a compass course is not only for long distances. It can be just as useful in a buoyed channel.

■ When you can see the next mark, it is usually easier to steer for it rather than steer a compass course. But, as you were reminded on the previous page, you have to be sure that the tide is not setting you off track.

Knowing where you are

It may seem obvious, but you as navigator must always know (or try to know) where you are. Among the good reasons for this are:

■ You need to know whether or not you are on your planned track.

■ You may want to check progress so that you can work out the time of arrival at your destination or the next point on your track.

■ You may want to change plans and head for a different destination.

Being able to know where you are is not usually a problem if you are close inshore or sailing in a buoyed channel.

You know where you are here!

■ *But the next project is finding your position when you are further out at sea.*

No doubt a GPS (if you have one) would solve the problem, but a navigator must also be able to find his position without the help of electronics.

Dead reckoning

In the next chapter you will learn how to find out your position by plotting bearings of objects on the shore.

But first you must learn to plot your position using a basic navigation ploy, which consists of working out where you *ought* to be.

Before we start, remember that plotting a course on your chart assumes that you know where you are starting from – for example a harbour entrance or the buoy at the end of a channel. This position is sometimes known as your *departure*.

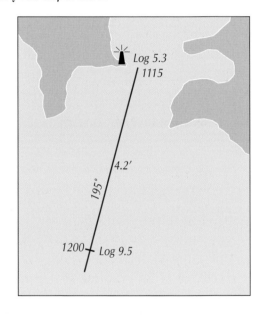

Suppose your log reads like this:

> 1115   *Lighthouse abeam close to starboard.*
>   *Log 5.3 Course 195˚*
>
> 1200 *Log 9.5*

Take the difference between the 1115 and 1200 log readings and at 1200 you find that you have sailed 4.2 miles. And your course was 195°.

    ...and your plotting looks like this ▶

This position on your chart at 1200 is your *dead reckoning* position – more usually known as your '1200 DR'.

A DR position is only a calculated position: it makes no allowance for the effects of the tide. But it is always valuable if you have nothing else. If you are doubtful, an up-to-date DR will show where you *ought* to be, and that may not be far from where you are.

So dead reckoning is a basic part of navigation. And it is a useful check (for instance on electronic navigation).

Plotting a series of up-to-date DR positions on your chart is known as '*keeping a DR*'.

> *Keeping your log book written up-to-date is essential, because an accurate DR depends on regular log readings, a record of courses steered and times of altering course. Some navigators like to put their log readings on the chart, but they should be entered in the log as well.*

The effect of the tide

We have said that dead reckoning takes no account of the tide.

In the diagram on the right is another simple example, this time taking account of the tide. We leave a mark again at 1115 and steer 135° until 1200 when a log reading is taken and the DR position is plotted. Assume that for the time and period the tidal stream atlas shows the stream flowing south at 1 knot. Therefore in our 45-minute passage we should have been set .75 south. This set is then applied to our 1200 DR and we have a 1200 estimated position (or EP) which has made allowance for the tide.

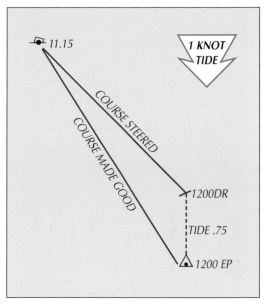

◀ *This is the symbol navigators use to indicate an estimated position.*

Allowing for the tide

In the example above, the EP showed you an estimation of how much the tide had set you off your intended track. But usually you will prefer to work out a course that will allow for the effects of the tide, so that you will end up on your intended track.

Here we are starting from **A** and we want to make good a course of 100°. But we know that there is a 1 knot set to the south. The boat's speed is estimated as 5 knots.

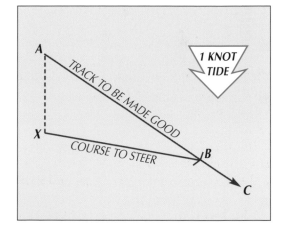

1. Draw the course to be made good (**AC**) (100°).
2. From point **A** plot one hour of tide (**AX**) – in this case 1 mile in the direction 180°.
3. Use dividers to measure the distance the boat will travel in one hour (5 miles) from **X** to where it meets the intended track at **B**. Then **XB** (082°) is the course to steer to make good 100°. **AB** – the distance covered in one hour – is the speed made good. Note that this working does require you to estimate your speed – which is not difficult.

CHAPTER 9

Fixing Your Position

Dead reckoning and estimated positions can be valuable but they are only calculated or estimated positions. Sailing along the coast the navigator can fix (which means 'establish') his position by plotting bearings of objects on the shore with a hand bearing compass.

Using a hand bearing compass

There are several types. The main use for a hand bearing compass is to take bearings of points on the shore. But it can also be used to take bearings of other vessels if there is a risk of collision.

Hand bearing compasses should be treated with care. When not in use, they should always be kept in their proper stowage.

■ If the compass has a lanyard, put it over your wrist or round your neck. Take care that you are looking at the object squarely so that you do get an accurate bearing.

■ You need a comfortable and secure position to take bearings. Standing in the main companion way is a good place – although you are not popular if you block the way for too long. If you have to stand on deck for a better view, stand somewhere comfortable and secure to anchor yourself.

Selecting objects for bearings:

■ These must be features that you can see, and which can be identified on the chart. The best bets are likely to be lighthouses, beacons, conspicuous buildings, isolated rocks and the edges of *bold* headlands (although these need not be high).

■ To start with, look at the coast, then look at the chart and decide which objects you are going to use, and write them in a notebook to plot on a chart afterwards. Write down the bearings as you take them and put the time alongside. As you should be able to take three bearings within a minute, a single time does for all your bearings.

Position lines

A single bearing of an object is known as a *position line or line of position (LOP)*. It is of limited value, because although you know that your position is along that line, you do not know where. However position lines may sometimes be better than nothing and they do have their uses.

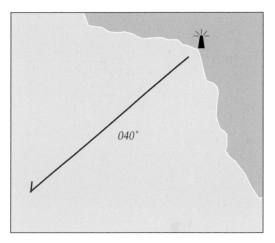

Fixes

But if you can take bearings of *two* objects, you can *fix* your position. You have a *two-point fix*.

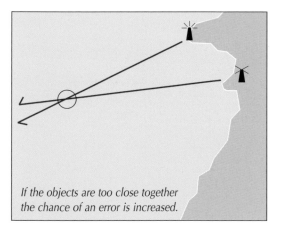

If the objects are too close together the chance of an error is increased.

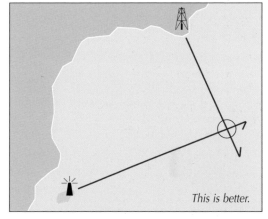

This is better.

But the more accurate result is likely to come from taking three (or more) bearings when you have a *three point* fix.

So your notebook looks something like this:

Lighthouse	002°	
Church	046°	
Pylon	092°	1145.

When you are writing down bearings |< and >| are useful abbreviations for 'right hand' and 'left hand edge' of headlands etc.

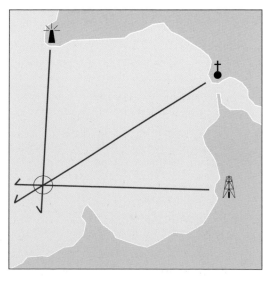

'Cocked hats'

But, unless you are lucky (or wishful thinking creeps into your plotting) your bearings will not meet tidily in the middle, as in the example on the previous page. You are more likely to end up with a *cocked hat* like this.

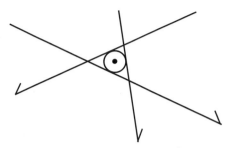

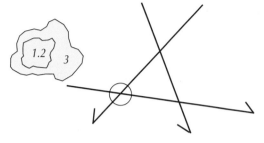

▲ *You normally take the middle of the cocked hat as your position.*

▲ *Unless you are near a danger, when you take the 'worst' position – the point nearest the danger.*

▶ *If the cocked hat is too big, there is far more chance of an error. You may have the bearing wrong, or mistaken the object on the shore. You can often realise which bearing is wrong by taking another look at them.*

The running fix

If only one fixing mark is available, you can still take a fix by using your log. In this example the boat is passing the headland on a course of 180°.

■ At 1115 a bearing of the lighthouse is taken and plotted. The log reading is noted.

■ At 1135 (allow a sufficient change of bearing to make a good cut) another bearing is taken and the log read. You have apparently advanced 1.4′ on your course of 180° since the first bearing.

■ This second bearing is plotted. Then using a ruler or plotter, advance the first bearing by 1.4′ in the direction 180° and you have a fix where both bearings cross.

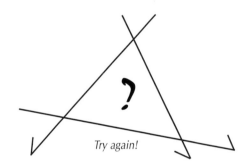

Try again!

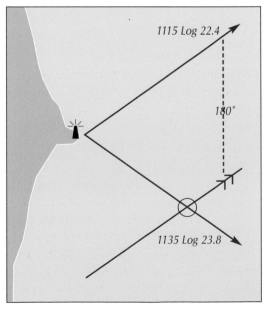

1115 Log 22.4

180°

1135 Log 23.8

Transits

When two objects are in line, they are said to be *in transit*. Transits can be very useful for the navigator – and there is no need for a compass bearing. You can have either natural or man-made features 'in transit'.

A pair of beacons in transit are used in some harbours as a guide to the entrance. These are known as *leading marks*, or *leading lights*, and are shown on the chart. The rear beacon or light is always the higher.

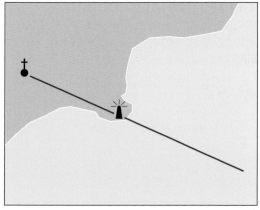

▲ *When the church spire and lighthouse are in line, this is a transit...*

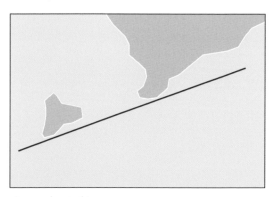

▲ *...and so is this.*

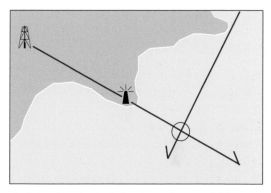

▲ *A transit and a single bearing makes a useful fix.*

The clearing bearing

This is more concerned with pilotage than with fixing your position, but it also means using your hand bearing compass. A single line of bearing can be useful to clear a danger – in which case it is called a *clearing bearing*.

If you are travelling on a course of 290° and you wait until the flagstaff bears 025° before turning into the bay, you will clear the shallow patch. This means that 025° is the clearing bearing to avoid the danger. You can plot this in advance.

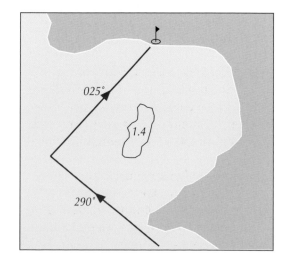

Going to windward – tacking

So far we have plotted courses on the assumption – if we are under sail – that the wind will be favourable and that we shall be able to steer the required course. But, of course, that does not always happen.

■ A working assumption for a modern cruising boat is that she can sail within 45° of the wind. This means that you can 'tack through 90°', and therefore, after you tack from one tack to the other, you will change course by approximately 90°.

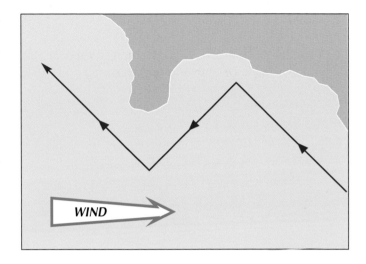

Sometimes you need just one short tack to get to windward of a mark. But when the next mark is almost dead to windward you may need several tacks. The tack that points you closest to your destination is known as the *favourable tack*.

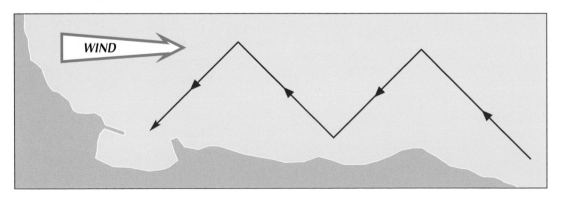

Racing yachts tend to tack frequently, taking care to be on the favourable tack and watching out for possible wind shifts. In general cruising yachts are more relaxed, and, wherever possible, make fewer tacks.

■ It is up to the navigator to advise when it is a good time to tack. When we are tacking to clear a mark we all tend to be optimistic and tack too early. A bearing with your hand bearing compass will be the best guide to the time to tack.

A simple passage

As a reminder of some of the points in this chapter and the last, let's follow a short section of an imaginary, but typical, coastal passage.

After rounding Sandy Point we have a 12 mile leg across Wide Bay before entering Oldport. The tidal stream chart shows the stream is weak.

The weather is hazy and there are no good fixing marks in Wide Bay, so it will be wise to keep plotting a DR position after passing Sandy Point.

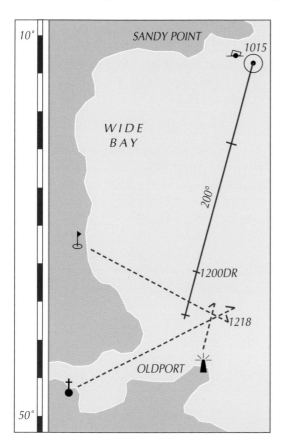

Being close to the buoy off Sandy Point gives a good position and a 'departure' for crossing the bay.

The log is 05.3 and the course is altered to 200°.

At 1100, the log reads 08.8. We have sailed 3.5 miles since the 1015 DR position was plotted.

1200. The log reads 13.2. A further DR is plotted.

1218. Visibility clears. A good three point fix taken shows us slightly to seaward of our DR position. Course is altered to head for the harbour entrance.

> **Note: *Once you have a good fix, you ignore your DR and start working from the new position.***

This very simple example emphasises two points:

■ It was only twelve miles across the bay and this might have been sailed without bothering to keep a DR plot. But, supposing the visibility had remained poor as you approached the coast, your DR position would have been very useful.

■ As you approach the coast, a good fix immediately gives you a firm position to work on.

CHAPTER 10

Into Harbour

It has been said that 'to travel hopefully is a better thing than to arrive.' Sailors will rarely agree – especially if it is starting to blow outside and there is the prospect of a nice sheltered anchorage. But the new navigator will usually be very content to arrive safely in a strange harbour.

For the small boat navigator a 'harbour' can be anything from a deserted Scottish loch to a narrow muddy creek, a rock-strewn harbour in Brittany or a busy commercial port. Some are perfectly easy to enter, others can present more of a challenge.

The key to to a peaceful arrival at any harbour (unless you know it well) is doing your homework – finding out as much information as possible beforehand.

There are many things about a harbour that are of interest to a visiting yacht, but which are not strictly the concern of the navigator – such as whether provisions are available, and what other facilities there are ashore. The factors that *do* concern the navigator particularly are:

- *The approach to the harbour, the entrance, and finding the way inside.*

- *The depth of the water inside (especially if it is a tidal harbour).*

Finding the information

There are three possible sources of information about a harbour, including how to enter it and what are the various facilities.

- The first and most important is your *chart*. There is both pilotage information and some details of shore facilities on the backs of some commercial charts.

- Then there is your *nautical almanac*. The amount of information varies but *Reeds Nautical Almanacs* cover virtually every harbour of any size in the UK and many in NW Europe. Local almanacs also deal with harbours in their area.

■ And there are the various *pilots* (sometimes called *cruising guides*). These are produced by commercial publishers and between them cover almost all the areas of the world visited by cruising yachtsmen. Some popular areas are covered by more than one author. Pilots are available in chandlers or sailing book shops.

Doing your homework

Study the chart of the harbour carefully to see what you can find out for yourself and then note information and advice from your almanac and any available pilot.

Some of the features to look for:

■ Can the place be easily identified when approaching? Some small harbours are not easy to recognize from seaward, although this may not be evident from the chart. Conspicuous landmarks can help, also photos or sketches in a pilot book.

■ Is there any shallow water at the entrance? Shallow entrances that are exposed to the open sea can be dangerous in certain weather conditions. The books warn about dangerous entrances, and there may also be warnings on the chart.

The chart of Aberdovey on the right is a good example.

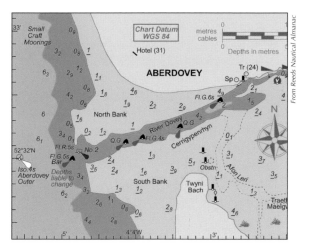

▲ *The approach channel to this harbour is well marked. But the bar across the entrance shows that it is difficult and could be dangerous in bad weather. The instructions confirm this.*

■ Is entry therefore possible in any weather?

■ Is entrance possible at any state of the tide?

■ Having entered the harbour, is there enough water to lie alongside or at anchor at any state of the tide?

■ What are the important navigation marks and are there any leading marks?

■ Are there any unmarked dangers?

■ Could you enter at night? Are there unlit buoys?

■ Almost every yacht has a VHF radio nowadays so that channels for calling anyone in the harbour for advice or assistance are worth noting in advance.

Depths inside

Many attractive smaller harbours are shallow and you will need your navigator's 'awareness of the tide'. In other words you must note the times of high and low water on the day you intend to visit, and the rise and fall on that day.

There may be times when you can use a harbour for a limited time around high water – for instance to take on fuel or water or pay a brief visit ashore. But if you plan to spend the night in a tidal harbour, you must ensure that, whether you will lie alongside, at a mooring, or at anchor, there will be enough water for your boat to lie afloat at low water – and allow a reasonable safety margin.

Information from almanacs

This extract from the section on Newhaven in the *Reeds Nautical Almanac* shows the the kind of information that is available (much use is made of abbreviations). Note the important warning about the entrance conditions in strong winds. A further section lists the telephone numbers of any local yachts clubs, boatyards, chandlers etc.

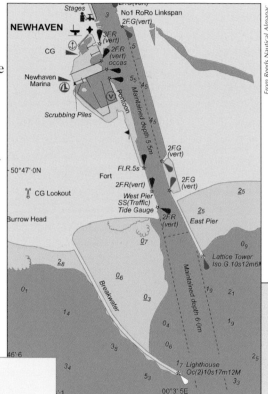

From Reeds Nautical Almanac

NEWHAVEN E. Sussex 50°46'.84N 00°03'.53E

SHELTER
Good in all weathers, but in strong on-shore winds there is often a dangerous sea at the entrance. Approach from the SW, to pass 50m off the breakwater head to avoid heavy breaking seas on the E side of the dredged channel. At marina (mostly dredged to to 2m), berth on inside of V pontoon, access 24 hours.

NAVIGATION
WPT 50°46'.24N 00°03'.60E, 168°/348° from/to W breakwater light, 0.32M. Caution: Harbour silts and dredging is continuous. Ferries/cargo vessels may warp off with hawsers across the harbour. Beware high speed ferries; check on VHF Ch 12.

LIGHTS & MARKS
Lighthouse on W breakwater is conspicuous. Traffic signs, displayed from tr on W side of river:

▼ over ●, or ● = Only entry permitted
● over ▼, or ● = Only departure permitted
●▼●(vert), or ●●● = No entry or departure
●or●●(vert) = Entry & departure permitted with care for vessels under 15m LOA.

HIGH SUMMIT

Pilots and cruising guides

The style varies according to the author and the publisher, but they are generally based on the expertise of active yachtsmen. These books can supply a lot of detail, both from the navigational aspect and facilities ashore. There are usually a number of charts which, while not intended as a replacement for navigational charts, often show local details more clearly. There are also photographs, including aerial photographs, which can be a great help in visualising what you see on the chart.

More importantly, these books can give you valuable advice on entering the more difficult harbours and anchorages, and also on making coastal passages.

Certainly some of this information is available in almanacs, but generally the cruising guides provide more detail. And for any navigator, whether new or experienced, they can be very helpful when visiting a harbour or anchorage for the first time. They are also useful for planning passages.

As a good example, the photograph below from *West Country Cruising Companion* by Mark Fishwick (Nautical Data Limited) gives a view of the Brisons, two rocky islets which provide a handy transit for the passage around Land's End inshore of the Longships Light. It certainly helps you to visualise the details shown on the chart. Incidentally this passage is for fine, calm weather, and daylight only.

▼ *The longships inshore passage marks: Brisons high summit just clear of low summit*

CAPE CORNWALL

LOW SUMMIT

Photograph by Mark Fishwick, West Country Cruising Companion, Published by Nautical Data/Yachting Monthly

Approaching harbour

■ We have already said that some harbours are hard to identify as they are approached from seaward, and conspicuous landmarks ashore are a help.

■ Before making the final approach, and particularly before getting into shallow water (check your echo sounder) try to establish a definite position on the chart. A channel buoy in the approach and clear of shallow water is a welcome check.

■ Never hesitate to stop and have a look. If you are not sure of your position and what is what on the shore, try to take a good fix, and plot it on your chart. From there you can plot a course to the entrance. It's safer than guessing.

■ Once the entrance has been sighted, check from the chart that you are approaching it on a safe course. Any leading marks are always a help.

■ Have your echo sounder running, and keep an eye on it.

▲ *The 25 metre daymark on Gribben Head in S. Cornwall does not have a light but its red and white stripes make a conspicuous landmark for the entrance to Fowey Harbour.*

Commercial ports

The ports used by ferries and other commercial vessels are usually easy to enter because they have deep, well marked approach channels and entrances.

■ Although it is not strictly a navigational matter, you do have to keep your eyes open (astern as well as ahead) for large vessels when you are sailing in the approaches to a commercial port. *And you do have to keep clear of them.*

The buoyed channels in these ports allow for deep draught vessels and you are advised, where possible, to sail just outside the edge of the channel (assuming always that you have checked the water depth on the chart). In fact certain ports (eg Harwich) do have an established yacht channel outside the main channel. This is shown on the chart.

■ Some busy ports with narrow entrances have traffic signals controlling the movement of vessels in and out. Watch out for these: the details will be found in your almanac.

■ Your almanac will also give you the VHF channel for making contact with the Harbour Master or port authorities.

...you do have to keep clear of them.

CHAPTER 11

Planning Passages

Even just 'going out for a sail' needs some thinking
ahead, if only noting the time of high water so that
you know what the tide is doing. A longer passage
does actually need planning.

Perhaps this chapter should have been called 'Being prepared' because weighing anchor or throwing off your lines and just 'pushing off' without some planning can mean that your day will not be as easy as it might be.

For a start:

■ Note the times of high and low water, whether there are spring or neap tides – or somewhere in between. Then see if the tide has any special effect on what you are planning to do.

■ Are there any places where the tidal streams are particularly strong, and where your timing may be affected? It could, in fact, affect leaving or returning to your own harbour. See *Tidal Gates* later in this chapter.

■ Check the weather and get an up-to-date forecast. This might be considered as the skipper's responsibility, but often the skipper is the navigator.

(Note: We are considering navigational matters here. Clearly there are other details that the skipper has to check before leaving harbour.)

Longer passages

A passage to another harbour (unless it is very close) does need some homework. Start with basic matters:

■ Have you got the right charts on board, including a large scale plan of any harbours to be visited? (You would not be the first navigator to discover half way through a passage that there was an important chart missing.)

■ How far is it? About how long is it going to take?

■ In a power boat, will you have enough fuel?

Planning is
helped by making brief
notes in a notebook or a
corner of your log. Here
is how they might look:

July 3
Yarmouth – Weymouth 39 miles
HW Portsmouth 0727 (neaps)
Tide is fair to Needles

St Albans – tide turns
foul at 1245
Weymouth HW 1338
LW 1836

Harbourmaster – channel 12
Harbour info. P/226.

■ What do you know about the harbour where you are planning to go? For instance, if you were delayed, would there be any problem about entering at night? (In the last chapter we looked at the sort of information you need to know about harbours, and where to find it.)

Now have a good look at the chart, then plot what seems to be the best route. It is helpful to write in the courses and distances, although the courses should be checked again when you are at sea.

■ Look again for any dangers such as rocks or shallow patches near where you are planning to go, and especially any that are *unmarked*. A danger is said to be *unmarked* when, although it is shown on the chart, it is not marked with a buoy, or some other navigational mark.

■ Having spotted any dangers, also look for things to help you such as buoys and lights.

■ Check the tidal streams from a tidal stream chart, and see whether you need make any allowance for them.

How far off?
When you are trying to plot a course along the coast, there is always the question of how far off the coast you should plan to sail and how closely you should round headlands.

There are often more rocks in the water to seaward of a rocky headland and sometimes, there are tide races. These cause broken water which is always uncomfortable for small craft, and sometimes dangerous. Tide races are usually shown on the chart and there may also be a warning. The broken water will be visible from your boat, so keep away from it.

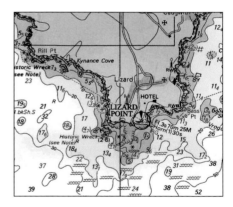

▲ *There are several formidable rocks off Lizard Head as well as a tide race that can be dangerous. It is a place to treat with respect.*

Shallow water often extends far off the end of low sandy points. (This also applies in rivers.)

As a general rule, plan to keep at least a mile or so offshore of the danger that is furthest from the shore, unless you need to be further out to avoid a tide race or keep clear of other dangers. Poor visibility, bad weather and a wind blowing towards the shore are all further reasons for giving the coast a wide berth. You can always edge in closer if the conditions look favourable and there are no dangers to avoid.

Shallow water

We are considering where you should or should not sail; so let's have another look at the question of shallow water. We talked about this briefly in Chapter 5 when you were learning to work out the exact height of the tide.

If, for instance, you are nosing your way into a sheltered creek (preferably on a rising tide), going slowly and watching your echo sounder, there is not much to worry about if there is only a metre or so under your keel, especially if the bottom is mud or sand.

But shallow patches in the open sea are quite different and to be avoided, especially in rough weather. The sea can break there, creating dangerous conditions for small craft (there is often a warning about this on the chart). Even if the sea is calm, a swell can make a shallow patch dangerous.

The example of Lath Rock is an *unmarked danger*. How far away from it should you be? In general terms, if you are sure of your position, perhaps from GPS or a good three point fix, half a mile might be reasonable.

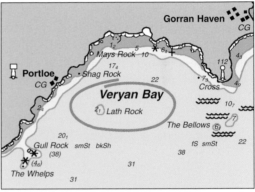

▲ *This is the sort of place to keep away from – even in calm weather.* **Note:** *The navigator has pencilled a ring to highlight a danger that might otherwise be overlooked.*

Time and the tide

Sailing yachts and some motor boats are relatively slow, and strong tidal streams can have a considerable effect on their progress – and their day's programme.

> *The less certain you are of your position, the further you should stay away from unmarked dangers.*

When you are cruising, the day's plan often starts with 'organisation' rather than navigation. For instance, although you might like to make an early start, you have to wait for fresh water before leaving your present harbour. But the crew would also like to arrive at your next port before the shops close, and so on.

Sometimes, of course, timing is straightforward. You have worked out the distance to your next destination, estimated your likely speed and there seems to be little tide to worry about, so an ETA (estimated time of arrival) is no problem. Although you realise that speed is never entirely predictable when you are depending on the wind.

But, especially around the UK, your route may take you through a point where the tidal stream is particularly strong. You need to get your timing right, and this is why these key points are often known as *tidal gates*.

Planning for the tide

Hurst Narrows in the West Solent (an area much used by small craft) is a classic example of a *tidal gate*. In the extract from the chart you will note the tidal stream diamond, and referring to the table, it shows that the stream can reach over 4 knots during spring

HIGH LIGHT Iso.WR.6s23M 14/11M

Hurst Point

Spoil Ground

Fort

		50° 42.1N 1° 32.7W	
		Rate *(kn)*	
Hours	Dir	Sp	Np
Before HW 6	049	3.7	1.9
5	053	3.9	1.9
4	055	3.5	1.8
3	057	3.5	1.7
2	064	2.5	1.2
1	263	0.2	0.1
HW	235	2.8	1.4
After HW 1	233	4.0	2.0
2	232	4.4	2.2
3	234	4.4	2.2
4	238	2.2	1.1
5	052	0.8	0.4
6	047	3.3	1.6

tides. Therefore any yacht planning to pass up and down the West Solent – or through any other tidal gate – will try to do so either at slack water or with a fair tide, so it is important to check your intended time of arrival here. After all even Shakespeare wrote about... *'catching the tide when it serves'.*

> *While looking at this area, it is worth mentioning 'wind against tide'. A fresh wind blowing against a strong tidal stream can cause an unpleasant, and sometimes dangerous sea. In the Needles Channel, a few miles SW of Hurst Narrows, a strong SW wind blowing against a spring ebb tide can certainly create dangerous conditions.*

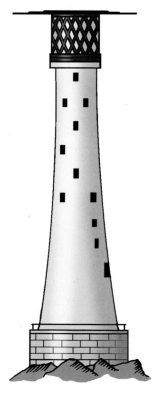

▶ *The Eddystone lighthouse is a splendid fixing mark – by night and by day. At night the light has a range of 24 miles. By day, the 41 metre tower (now with a heli-copter platform on top) stands alone in the open sea, and is conspicuous from a long distance.*

Knowing where you are

■ On coastal passages, look for marks that can be used for taking fixes.

■ Further offshore (or in poor visibility) when taking fixes from points on the shore is not possible, you will need to keep a DR. Check that your log is working so that regular log readings can be taken.

■ Have your tidal atlas marked with the appropriate times of high water and be ready to plot any effects of the tidal stream on your DR.

■ When you approach the shore again, you will be looking for landmarks to check your position.

Even if you are using GPS it is still sensible to check your position against an occasional shore fix, or DR if you are offshore.

54

CHAPTER 12

More About Your Compass

*In Chapter 3 we had a brief look at the compass,
and at magnetic variation. We now need to add
more detail. It may not be a fascinating subject, but it
is an important one to understand.*

Magnetic versus true

Let's sum up what we have covered already:

■ In Chapter 3 we saw that the *magnetic compass* points to *magnetic north* (as opposed to true north) and that the difference between *true* north and *magnetic* north is known as *magnetic variation*.

■ But we suggested that, if using a plotter, you work only with magnetic courses and bearings.

However, just as you have been working with *magnetic* courses and bearings, there can, of course, be *true* courses and bearings, and there may be times when you do have to work with them. And as you progress as a navigator you will need to learn how to convert *true* courses to *magnetic*, and vice versa.

Converting magnetic to true – or true to magnetic

The simplest way to do this is to use your plotter.

1. Pencil the variation on to your plotter.

2. To convert a magnetic bearing – rotate the protractor disc to line up with your pencil mark and read the answer in True from the 0 centreline.

3. To convert a true bearing – rotate the protractor disc to line up with the 0 centreline and read the answer in magnetic from the pencilled mark.
   This is trickier to explain than it is to do!

Deviation

Any metal object brought near the compass may affect it. One of the main risks was said to be the sailor's knife, but nowadays mobile phones, or cameras with electronic flash attachments are much more likely to upset the compass. The crew sometimes need reminding about this.

These are portable items that can be kept away from the compass, but most yachts have a large hunk of metal – their engine – sited not far from their steering compass. The error induced in the compass by the engine, and anything else in the hull or in the electrical system is called the *compass deviation*.

■ *Deviation* is the angle between magnetic north and north as indicated by your compass. It is a local error in your boat.

■ If the compass points to the east of magnetic north – then it is said to have easterly deviation.

> *Unlike variation which is constant whatever your heading, deviation changes with the vessel's heading.*

Deviation need not be a problem because, in most yachts, it can be almost eliminated.

Compensating magnets can be placed near the compass, and these can usually reduce deviation to a minimum, or remove it altogether.

As compass courses are rarely steered to within an accuracy of a couple of degrees, a degree or two of deviation is not going to cause a serious error – at least over short distances. So in most boats it is feasible to ignore deviation.

This process of placing and adjusting these magnets is known as *swinging the compass*. This should be done, usually by a professional *compass adjuster*, when vessels are new, and after major refits or work that might affect the compass.

DEVIATION CARD

Boat __Stella Lyra__

Date __06.05.98__

Magnetic course	Deviation	Compass course
000	2° E	358
030	2° E	028
060	1°E	059
090	0	090
120	1° W	121
150	1° W	151
180	2° W	182
210	1° W	211
240	0	240
270	0	2700
300	1° E	299
330	1° E	329

Even if the deviation is negligible the compass adjuster produces a *deviation card*, showing the deviation on each heading. and this card should be displayed over the chart table.

Correcting for deviation

If you find yourself in a boat with deviation that you cannot ignore, then you do have to allow for it.

> **Make use of an old sailors' rule:**
> *Deviation east – compass least*: Deviation is *subtracted* from the magnetic course.
>
> *Deviation west – compass best*: Deviation is *added* to the magnetic course.

The 'CADET' rule

Converting magnetic courses to true, and vice versa is perfectly simple by calculation. You just have to remember which way the variation should be applied. The 'east – least' and 'west – best' rule quoted above also works for variation, but the 'CADET' rule also works well.

■ Remember that, in this instance, compass is the same as magnetic.

> *C A D E T*
> **Compass to true – add east**

To convert a *compass* course to a *true* course add *easterly* variation and therefore subtract *westerly* variation.

To convert *true* to *compass* – reverse the process, which means subtract *easterly* and add *westerly* variation.

For example:

1. If the true course is 045°, and the variation is 5° E, what is the magnetic (compass) course?

> *True to compass, add west – so subtract east.*
> *Compass course is 040°.*

2. If the magnetic (compass) course is 130° and the variation is 11° E, what is the True course?

> *Compass to true, add east.*
> *True course is 141°.*

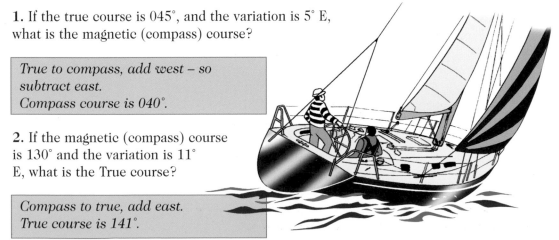

CHAPTER 13

Sailing at Night

Even if you have not planned it, you may soon find that you are sailing after dark, perhaps because of a failing wind – or a failed engine. So you have to be able to cope.

In the same way that you will be wise to avoid rough weather at the start, you had better begin by practicing your navigation in the daylight.

But navigation at night is not difficult. And in some ways it is easier than by day because lights can be identified at a distance by their flashes. In fact it is said that the best time to reach port after an offshore passage is at dawn. You have been able to identify the coast by a light or lights in the dark hours, but you have daylight to find your way into harbour.

The hardest time after dark can be when you are in a busy area like the Solent or the Straits of Dover. With the lights ashore, the lights of ships, and the flashing lights of numerous buoys, it can look rather bewildering. But there is an answer.

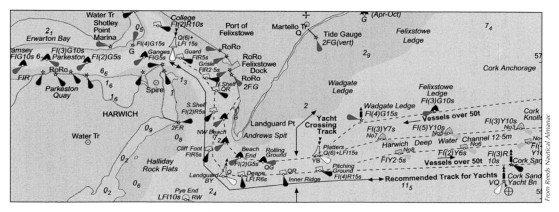

From Reeds Nautical Almanac

▲ *This helpful chart from Reeds Nautical Almanac shows that the approach to Harwich and Felixstowe is an area that might look challenging at night. There are nearly thirty lit buoys outside the entrance as well as those inside. There will be busy commercial traffic, and numerous shore lights in the background. Note the recommended track for small craft outside the big ship channel.*

Busy areas at night

If you find yourself in a situation like the one illustrated opposite outside Harwich it is not difficult to find your way if you follow these rules:

1. Make sure that you start from a certain position – for instance close to a buoy that you have identified. (If in any doubt, shine a light on it and read the name!)

2. Plot a track to your destination, staying inside or close to buoyed channels. Avoid short cuts. Note courses and distances between marks. If possible do this in advance.

3. As you proceed:
   – identify buoys carefully.

   – keep track of your progress, so that you *always know where you are*.

4. Keep a good lookout for other ships – not forgetting to look astern.

And so, even if the horizon does look like Piccadilly Circus, following these simple rules carefully should make things safe and easy – especially if you have studied the chart beforehand.

Identifying lights

Even if a light appears where and when you expect it,
always *check its flashes (its chacteristic).*

A stop watch is not easy at night, but a useful way of counting seconds is to say:
ONE THOUSAND, TWO THOUSAND, THREE THOUSAND *etc.*

So, if the chart says that a light is flashing twice every ten seconds, you should expect to see two flashes while you count ten seconds.

Night vision

When you are sailing at night the lighting below decks must be kept as low as possible. This is very important for the navigator. If you have been working on a lighted chart table, you cannot expect to be able to see properly when you come on deck. Chart tables need a dimmed light for use at sea, and cabin lights must be switched off or shaded.

It is often better for the navigator to carry a small pocket torch (shaded if necessary) and use that to look at the chart.

Compass lights, which should be red, are often too bright for comfort, even if they are fitted with a dimmer. Red nail varnish on the bulb helps.

CHAPTER 14

Becoming a Navigator

*Navigation certainly means learning some
theory, but it is very much a practical skill. Here is advice on a
few practical matters for the would-be navigator.*

Checking your compass

There is a saying that 'you must always be able to rely on your compass' – and so you must. You would be lost (literally) without it. Once in a while compasses do go haywire. Perhaps someone has stowed their camera (with electronic flash) or their mobile phone in a corner near the compass binnacle, or there has been a change in the boat's electrics.

> Take every opportunity of checking your compass. Even a rough check is better than none.
>
> An easy way is to compare the steering compass with the hand bearing compass. It is best if the person holding the hand bearing compass stands right aft. This is only approximate, but it should show up any serious error.
>
> Another more accurate method is to line the boat up on a transit whenever there is the opportunity, for instance when entering a harbour where there are leading marks you can read the correct bearing from the chart.

Rough weather

If you go to sea in small boats, you may avoid bad weather for most of the time, but not entirely. However, the navigator's job is still the same in rough weather, and it can be uncomfortable. For instance, trying to plot on a small chart table that is heeled over at 30 degrees is less easy than practising your chart work on the dining room table. And if you have ever been seasick you will know only too well that it can be difficult to concentrate, which the navigator must do.

So when you first start navigating, it may be wise to avoid rough weather unless you really do have a strong stomach. Stay in harbour or let someone else take over. But as you become more experienced, take a look at the problems of navigating in bad weather and decide to cope with them. Thousands of navigators do.

Logs (log books)

Navigators tend to have personal ideas about keeping a log. For a start it can either be kept in an exercise book, or else in a printed log book designed for the purpose.

Although some sailors like to write up a detailed cruise log, it is the navigation log that concerns us here. It is a general rule, often not followed, that you should be able to plot a vessel's position entirely from her log entries.

You were reminded in Chapter 7 that regular log entries are essential for dead reckoning. And, allowing that the navigator may need to rest or sleep on a long day at sea, he must remind the crew to make any necessary entries in the log, such as the time of altering course or tacking, together with the log reading at that time.

On passage, when a compass course is being steered, the helmsman must be encouraged to enter the course *that he has actually been able to steer* (important when going to windward) rather than the intended course. This should be done at the end of each hour.

From: *Dartmouth*		Towards: *Salcombe*		And at:		Date: *June 24*	
Time	Course		Log	Remarks		Wind	Bar
	Ordered	Steered					
08.00				Forecast SE 3-4 Vis good			1003
8.35				Slipped from dock			
08.42				Homestead buoy abeam Course 175°		SSE3	
09.20	175°		04.2	Sterries buoy abeam stbd. 5 mile A/C 200°			
10.05	200°	205°	08.3	Start Point light bears 270° A/C 245°			
10.45	270°		12.4	Pawle Point lt. bears 355° A/C 320°			
11.25			15.4	Entering Salcombe Harbour			
11.50			16.7	picked up mooring off Salcombe Y.C.			
Date:		Distance run: 16.7		Engine hours run: 1.2		Fuel remaining: 4 gals	

▲ *This is the sort of detail that it is useful to enter in your log. Weather information should always be included. Note: A/C is the usual abbreviation for alter course.*

The right course

Whenever you ask the helmsman to steer a course, insist (politely) that they repeat it so that you know it has been understood. Many sailors do this by custom, but mistakes and misunderstandings can happen.

Keeping charts up to date

It may be hard to understand why your charts do need keeping up to date, and why, from time to time, new editions are issued. After all, the Needles or Land's End don't move. But in shallow areas like the Thames Estuary the position of the sand banks can certainly change, and this means that buoys have to be moved.

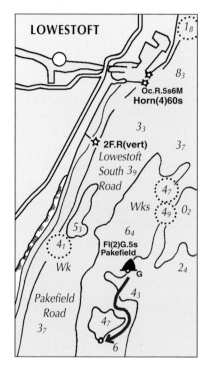

This extract from the chart showing the approaches to Lowestoft has been corrected, and it shows two buoys that have been moved more than half a mile because of shifting sandbanks. This correction was published some years ago, but it is a good example.

If you had been approaching Lowestoft with an old or uncorrected chart you would, at best, have found this confusing. But at night or in bad weather you might have run aground and been in serious trouble.

The buoys' new positions after the chart has been corrected.

There can be other changes too. For example a new marina is built or a new jetty in a harbour. Or, in some areas, obstructions like fish farms or oil rigs are moved. All this is confusing for the navigator if he does not find the changes on his chart. New and up-to-date editions of Leisure Charts are normally published annually, but corrections to Admiralty charts are available free of charge on the internet (www.nmwebsearch.com). However, corrections to Leisure Charts have to be referred to the number of the standard Admiralty chart on which the Leisure Chart is based. This is shown on the bottom left-hand corner.

Another convenient source of UK chart corrections is in the magazine *Practical Boat Owner*. Regular corrections to commercial charts are also available. Details are shown on the chart.

■ When you use someone else's charts look at their date or the date of the last correction (usually in the bottom left hand corner). Be cautious if they are old and uncorrected.

There is no doubt that you can get away with old or uncorrected charts – for a time! But it can be an uncomfortable moment when you discover that your chart is no longer up to date.

Taking care of charts

Charts are expensive and need looking after. Admiralty charts are flat, usually folded in two, although they may be rolled up when they are first supplied. They should be unrolled and kept flat. On board, if there is not enough room for a chart drawer under the chart table, a convenient stowage is under a bunk cushion.

Charts in Admiralty Leisure Folios are flat, but other types of chart are folded up like a road map. Take care to fold them back in the same way when you have finished with them.

Use a soft pencil such as 2B for chart work and have a good quality soft eraser to clean off the old tracks and workings before a chart is stowed away – unless there is a reason for keeping them. If they are left on the chart it is easy to mistake old workings for new.

Check... and check again

You have already been reminded to check the identity of buoys and marks as you pass them. And this is not only when you are in a buoyed channel.

Suppose, for instance, that you are sailing where there are numerous buoys, but they are spaced well apart, like parts of the East Coast.

You will be pleased when the next mark does appear at the expected time and in just about the right place. Good! But don't forget to get your binoculars out and check the name or number because – just very occasionally – it won't be the buoy you are expecting. Perhaps the tide has been stronger than you expected. If ever this does happen to you try to find out *what caused the error*, so that it will not happen again.

But checking is more than just identifying marks.

- *'Did I look up the right day in the tide tables?'*
- *'Did I plot the course correctly on the chart?'*
- *'Is the ETA at the next mark right?'*

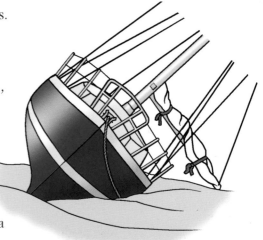

This is not to say that you start your navigating in a permanent state of uncertainty. But it never hurts to check. Mistakes are easy, and checking does not mean a lack of self-confidence. Any marine insurance company will tell you stories of navigators – more experienced than you – who *didn't* check.

▲ *A navigator who didn't check?*

CHAPTER 15

Electronic Navigation

Electronic navigation is now used, at least to some degree, on most boats. It ranges from hand-held GPS sets that just give latitude and longitude to chart plotters that show the boat's position on a screen with a chart similar to a paper chart. You must understand the principles of GPS and how it can aid small craft navigation.

GPS – what it is
The Global Positioning System (GPS) gets its information from a series of satellites in orbit around the globe, and presents its data in the form of the latitude and longitude on the receiver. The information is constantly updated and the more complex the receiver, the more information it can give the navigator.

GPS and the new navigator

GPS, often combined with an electronic plotter, is an important part of modern small craft navigation – although not every boat carries one. But it would be wrong for the would-be navigator to think 'Well, I've got GPS so I don't need to know much about regular navigation.' Because using GPS efficiently does need a knowledge of basic navigation.

What is a waypoint?
Before looking further at GPS, it is essential to understand what a waypoint is.
A waypoint can be a position such as a harbour entrance or a buoy, or a latitude and longitude position that you can enter into your GPS. This can then give you a course to steer from your present position to the required waypoint.

■ When entering waypoints ensure that you have entered the right one. If using latitude and longitude have you entered the correct figures? If it is a buoy, have you identified the right one? A good check is to compare the bearing and distance on your paper chart!

■ Remember that your GPS works in a straight line and gives the direct course from one waypoint to another. It does not give left and right turns like a car navigator. *Always check that there are no hazards that may lie in between the two waypoints.*

Hand-held GPS sets

As the price of receivers has fallen, a hand-held GPS set is often used as a back-up in case of any problems with the main set. They usually accept waypoints as well as giving you your position and boat speed over the ground.

◄ *Hand-held GPS sets have become very popular.*

► *The Garmin 298 GPS is a very popular fixed unit for the small boat navigator.*

Fixed GPS sets

These are fixed to the boat either near the helm or the chart table and run off the boat's main electrical supply. They can be programmed with waypoints; storing up to 500 waypoints is usual, but some can store as many as 3000.

Chart Plotters

These have the addition of a chart on the screen which displays all the details shown on a paper chart such as lights, buoys, depth of water, port information, as well as the position of the vessel. It is important when fitting the plotter to ensure that the screen can easily be seen in various conditions of daylight. There is an increasing selection of electronic charts available in the form of chips that fit the plotter.

▲ *The Garmin 2210 electronic chart plotter.*

Man overboard

Most GPS sets have an MOB key. In the event of a person falling from the boat, press the MOB key and the set will give you a display showing the course and distance back to the casualty.

Radar

Radar sets and radomes have become smaller and lighter; ideal for smaller boats. Radar works by sending out a beam which is reflected back to the boat, and any land, buoys, ships etc which are caught by the radar beam appear on the radar screen.

An important use of radar nowadays is to avoid collisions with other ships, and anyone who has been caught in fog in an area with heavy traffic will be very glad to have radar on board. But radar can be used for navigation as well.

Images of buoys, lighthouses, and stretches of coastline can be seen on radar. In poor visibility it can show the way up buoyed channels and indicate harbour entrances. But to get the best out of radar, a certain amount of skill and experience is needed both to adjust the set and to identify targets on the display.

As might be expected, radar gives a more accurate view of a steep coast than a low lying one. If the coast is low, you may be seeing echoes from higher land further inshore. Radar tends to give more accurate ranges than bearings so, for instance, a radar range of the Eddystone Lighthouse combined with a visual bearing would provide a good fix.

▶ The Skerryvore lighthouse, off the Western Isles of Scotland, has a Racon. Its signal shows on a radar screen to warn of fearsome rocks.

The 'Man Overboard' button (MOB) on a GPS receiver.

Read the Instruction Book
Before using any equipment on board, especially navigation equipment, READ THE BOOK. A little time spent understanding the set and how it works will give you the confidence to use the equipment well, and it is better to learn on the quiet of your mooring rather than out at sea.

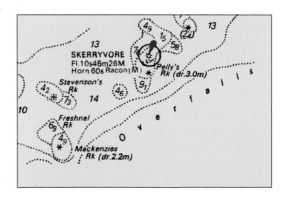

CHAPTER 16

Are You Ready to Navigate?
– a Summary

Before you leap into your boat and disappear out of the harbour, we suggest that you work through this final chapter, and then have a look back at anything that is still not quite clear.

Note: *Figures in brackets refer to chapter numbers.*

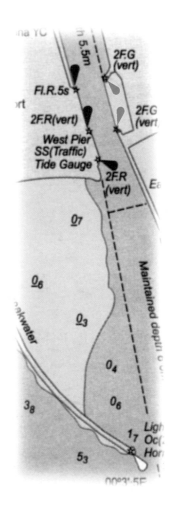

Charts (1)
You know what types of charts are available. And when you look at a chart you understand just about everything that you see on it, including: the latitude and longitude, chart symbols, and soundings. You know where to look up anything that you do not understand.

> *In a word, you are happy using charts.*

Buoys and Lights (2)
You can recognize the various types of buoy, both on the chart and when you see them on the water. So you could recognize the difference between a *starboard hand buoy* and a *cardinal buoy*, and you know their purposes.

You know what a light's *characteristic* is, and could tell the difference between a *flashing* and an *occulting* light.

Your Compass (3)
You understand what is meant by *magnetic variation* but have been encouraged to work with *magnetic* courses and bearings only – at least for the moment. You know that at sea, 'direction' can either be a *course* or a *bearing*.

Working on a Chart (4)

You know how to use dividers to measure distance, and what a *compass rose* is. And you can plot courses and bearings with either a parallel ruler or a plotter.

Do you remember how a vessel's or an object's position can be stated, and can you plot a given latitude and longitude?

You understand the relation between time, speed and distance, and can use the tables to work this out.

> *You have been able to practice plotting on a chart with either a plotter or a parallel ruler. So you can now plot courses and bearings reasonably quickly.*

Tides – Rising and Falling (5)

Do you understand *high water* and *low water*, and know how often they usually occur? What are *springs* and *neaps*?

You know what tide tables are for and how to use them. And you know how to work out the time and height of high and low water at a port for which there are no detailed tide tables.

Why is it sometimes necessary to know the times of high and low water accurately as well as the height of the tide?

Tidal Streams (6)

You understand about the tide flooding and ebbing. And you know what tidal stream charts are, where to find them, and how to use them.

> *These two chapters have made you 'tide conscious'.*
> *You realise now just how important the tide is, and why you must always be aware of what it is doing.*

Navigation Instruments (7)

You know what the log and the echo sounder can be used for and how they help you as a navigator.

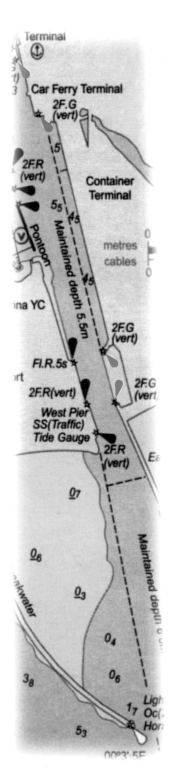

Getting Started (8)

This is where you learned about putting into practice some of the theory that you have learned so far. Do you understand what is meant by *pilotage* or 'buoy hopping' and why you need to be careful in what seems a very easy way of getting around?

Although it may have seemed obvious, do you remember why the navigator should always know where he is? What is meant by *dead reckoning*, and can you plot a *DR* position? What is an *estimated position* or *EP*? Can you plot one?

Fixing Your Position (9)

You know how to use a hand bearing compass and choose suitable objects for taking a fix, and you know about *two* and *three point fixes,* and *cocked hats.*

Do you remember what a *transit* is?

> *Being able to take a fix and put it on the chart quite quickly is a basic navigator's skill. It needs practice, but is not difficult.*

Into Harbour (10)

You were reminded that entering harbour, especially where you have not been before, does need preparation. This information can be obtained from your chart, from your almanac, and from a pilot. Do you remember the things that the navigator must be most concerned about?

What does the navigator have to consider when approaching a harbour?

Planning Passages (11)

You were reminded that it is not only a passage between two ports that needs planning, but any trip to sea needs some forethought.

Do you remember the advice about how far off you should sail from headlands, and how to keep clear of dangers?

What is a *tidal gate* and why might it affect your day's programme?

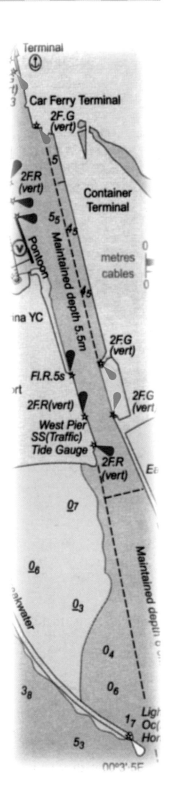

More About Your Compass (12)

Perhaps not an easy chapter, but a part of basic navigation that you do need to understand.

Having so far worked only with magnetic bearings and courses, you now know about using true courses. And this means being able to convert *magnetic* into *true*, and vice versa.

Do you know what *deviation* is, what causes it, and what happens when a compass is *swung*?

Do you remember the **CADET** rule?

Sailing at Night (13)

You doubtless will plan not to navigate at night – at least to start with. But you may have to cope and this gives some advice on how. In particular what should you do if you find yourself after dark in an area with numerous lights and navigation marks, and commercial shipping as well?

Becoming a Navigator (14)

In this mixed bag of practical advice, there was a word of caution about starting your navigation in rough weather.

Do you now realise that charts may need correcting and why using out-of-date charts could be dangerous?

You were given some ideas about keeping a log. Do you know what you should be including?

Finally have you understood the importance of checking your navigational work all the time?

Electronic Navigation (15)

Although electronic navigation is playing an increasing part in yacht navigation, it still needs a knowledge of basic navigation.

In this chapter you had a brief look at GPS, plotters and radar, and found out what they are and what they can do.

You are starting to know what it can do – and what it can't.

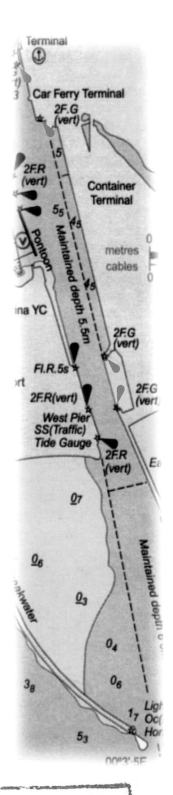

Glossary

General glossary

Beacon. An unlit navigation mark. Can be either a pole with a topmark on a sandbank or a more substantial structure ashore.

Bearing. The direction of one point, ashore or afloat, from another.

Cardinal points. North, east, south and west.

Characteristic. The distinctive pattern of flashes used to identify a light.

Cocked hat. The triangle resulting from three bearings that do not meet exactly at one point.

Course. The direction in which a vessel is pointing or heading.

Course made good. The direction in which a vessel is travelling 'across the chart' or over the ground. Not necessarily the same as the course she is steering.

Dead reckoning (DR). A calculated position based on a boat's course and distance travelled in a given time.

Deviation. The compass error caused by a vessel's engine(s) and other metal or electrical items near the compass. Technically it is the angle between magnetic north and north as shown by the compass.

Estimated position (EP). A DR position (see above) adjusted for known or estimated *tidal stream* or *leeway*.

Fix. Theoretically this is a vessel's position plotted by any means, but usually in small boats it is a position achieved by taking bearings of objects ashore. (Also used as a verb to *fix* your position.)

GPS (Global Positioning System). An electronic navigation system used by small craft (and others) using information from satellites.

Heading. The direction in which the bow of a boat is pointing at any time.

Latitude. The measurements of a vessel's position north or south of the Equator.

Leading lights. A pair of lights *in transit* used to show the passage into a harbour.

Leading marks. As above, but unlit.

Leeway. Slight sideways movement of a boat through the water, caused by the effect of the wind.

Log. A device for measuring distance travelled through the water.

Log (log book). A book for writing navigation information and other details of a vessel's activities.

Longitude. The measurements of a vessel's position east or west of Greenwich (which is longitude 0°).

Magnetic north. The direction of the Magnetic North Pole. The direction in which the needle of a magnetic compass points (apart from errors).

Mark. A fixed feature on the chart that can be used to identify a vessel's position. Buoys, beacons etc are known as *navigation marks*.

Meridian. A line of longitude.

Pilot (book). A nautical guide book giving details of coastlines and harbours and instructions for entering them.

Position line (or LOP). A single line, indicating a vessel's position, somewhere on the line. The result of taking a single bearing of an object ashore.

Range. The distance at which a light on a lighthouse may be seen by a ship. Also the distance of an object detected by radar.

Running fix. A fix using two bearings of a single object on the shore and based on the distance run between the two bearings.

Sounding. A depth of water, usually referring to depths shown on the chart.

Topmark. A distinctive shape secured to the top of a buoy or beacon to aid identification.

Track. The path you plot on a chart and intend to follow.

Transit. Two objects in line, as seen by the observer.

True north. The direction of the True North Pole. It is always at the top of the chart, indicated by lines of longitude.

Variation. The angle between true north and magnetic north in any place.

Tidal glossary

(There are so many words connected with the tide and tidal streams that it is useful to give them a separate glossary.)

Actual depth. The actual depth of water at any point. It is found by adding the tidal height (from tide tables) to the charted depth.

Chart datum. The reference point to which heights and depths on the chart are referred. It is also the lowest point to which the tide is ever expected to fall.

Charted depth. The depth shown on the chart of the sea bed at that point. The depth below *chart datum*.

Duration of the tide. The time between high water and the previous low water–normally just over 6 hours.

Drying height. The height (above chart datum) of any ground that is uncovered at low water.

Ebb. The movement of the tide after high water, when it is flowing out.

Flood. The movement of the tide as it moves in towards high water, when it is rising.

Height (of the tide). A figure obtained from tide tables showing the height of the tide above chart datum.

Making. The tidal range at neaps is small, and larger at springs. As the range increases from neaps to springs the tide is said to be *making*. The opposite is *taking off*.

Neap tides (neaps). Tides when the rise and fall is smallest, occuring at the first and last quarters of the moon. The opposite to *spring tides*.

Range. The difference in the height of successive high and low waters. The amount the tide is rising and falling at any time.

Secondary Port. A port for which there may not be detailed tide tables, and where the tides are worked out in relation to a *Standard Port*.

Set. The direction in which a tidal stream or current moves.

Slack water. The period around high water and low water when the movement of the tide is minimal.

Spring tides (springs). The tides occurring around the times of full moon and new moon, when the rise and fall (the range) is largest and the tidal stream runs most strongly.

Standard Port. One of the limited number of ports for which tidal predictions in almanacs and tide tables are given in full. Can be used for calculations at *Secondary Ports*.

Taking off. The opposite to 'making'. (See above.)

Tidal gate. An area where the tidal stream is strong, where timing may be crucial to avoid a strong foul tide.

Tidal race. An area of confused and sometimes dangerous water caused by the effect of the tidal stream off headlands or in narrow passages.

Tidal stream. The horizontal movement of the tide, as opposed to its rising and falling.

Index